"It takes a contemplative soul f   ·   ·-·-l -+ once
scholarly and poetic to render
and beauty. This book offers sı
the wilderness."

G000078697

    —Erik Varden
      Mount Saint Bernard

"With *Clothed in Language* Pauline Matarasso has written a
modern Wisdom book. If much of the biblical Wisdom literature
teaches a person how to act, Matarasso offers numinous insights
into how *to be*. Just as importantly, she pushes aside the iron
curtain of the Enlightenment and modern Scientism, with their
excessive emphasis on rationalism, in order to show us how to
learn—or relearn—and use theological imagination. Many of her
brief reflections remind me of the *apophthegmata*, the sayings of
the early Christian monks, the abbas and ammas of the desert.
This book will last. It is a good book for *lectio*—whether in
refectory, office, school, or the quiet place Jesus tells us to go to
when we pray."

    —Tim Vivian
      Professor Emeritus of Religious Studies
      California State University, Bakersfield

"Wise, insightful, provocative, mystical, potentially
transformative. Pauline Matarasso's meditative, poetic prose
immerses the reader in the mysteries of God's manifestation
through the Word, inviting the reader to pay closer attention
to the relationship between language and the experience of the
divine."

    —Elizabeth Thompson
      Associate Professor of English
      Ohio University

MONASTIC WISDOM SERIES: NUMBER FIFTY-NINE

Clothed in Language

Pauline Matarasso

α

Cistercian Publications
www.cistercianpublications.org

LITURGICAL PRESS
Collegeville, Minnesota
www.litpress.org

A Cistercian Publications title published by Liturgical Press

Cistercian Publications
Editorial Offices
161 Grosvenor Street
Athens, Ohio 45701
www.cistercianpublications.org

Scripture texts in this work are taken from the New Jerusalem Bible, the Revised Standard Version, and the Grail Psalms.

Library of Congress Cataloging-in-Publication Data

Names: Matarasso, Pauline Maud, author.
Title: Clothed in language / Pauline Matarasso.
Description: Collegeville, Minnesota : Cistercian Publications, [2019]
 | Series: Monastic wisdom series ; number fifty-nine | Includes
 bibliographical references.
Identifiers: LCCN 2019010762 (print) | LCCN 2019022352 (ebook) |
 ISBN 9780879071592 (ebook) | ISBN 9780879070595 (pbk.)
Subjects: LCSH: Language and languages—Religious aspects—
 Christianity—Biography. | Metaphor—Religious aspects—Christianity.
 | Matarasso, Pauline Maud.
Classification: LCC BR115.L25 M38 2019 (print) | LCC BR115.L25
 (ebook) | DDC 230.01/4—dc23
LC record available at https://lccn.loc.gov/2019010762
LC ebook record available at https://lccn.loc.gov/2019022352

To the Community of Mount Saint Bernard
who opened to me
the doors of their hearts;
and remembering specially
John Morson and Hilary Costello, OCSO,
who shared with me so freely the treasures of the Fathers.
1973–2019

Contents

Acknowledgments

I remember here the long line of those who have walked with me down the years in kinship and in friendship, the known and the nameless, those who are still beside me and the greater crowd already beyond.

First and always I remember those who have pointed me towards that beyond, by word or by example.

I remember those who gave me a love of learning, and languages in which to listen to other voices—especially the clear tones of those lying mute in archives, waiting to be given back their speech.

I remember the headmistress who read Dickens to twelve-year-olds and wrote to me years later, "I always believed in you."

I remember Helen Waddell, who led me, at seventeen, into the Middle Ages to meet the cloud of witnesses of whom Wulfric of Haselbury and John of Forde still hold me by the hand.

I remember the poets whom I carry around with me: W. S. Graham, Marie Noël, Ruth Pitter, Charles Péguy, Charles Causley, and the many others who come visiting.

I remember all who have shown me kindness and understanding, and made me laugh.

I remember those I have forgotten.

All these have helped me on the way and have a part in this book, and to all I say, Thank You.

To those who have played a more immediate part in its genesis, I owe a more specific gratitude, and first to Catherine Wybourne, who gave the initial push and has stood behind it from then on; to my son François, who keeps the show on the road in more senses than one; to Eric Southworth, Martin Laird, OSA, and Gabriel Everitt, OSB, for steadfast encouragement; to Erik Varden, OCSO, for his caring and vigilant reading of the text, and the refinements that resulted, and lastly to Marsha Dutton, of Cistercian Publications, who has seen it through the editorial process with much sensitivity and patience.

Clothed in Language

Sighing and Prophesighing

Sighing and prophesighing
before the God who was in the beginning
and is and ever may be,
in whom we believe and doubt
and think and feel and yearn and imagine,
in whom we strive and fail,
to whom we travel and from whom we run;
the God who is the non-sense to the far north
of paradox,
who holds in balance now and never
and for ever,
who makes of self and other
one.

The Word for whom we spread our nets of metaphor
to capture our heart's hart leaping on the mountains,
looking through the lattice
of our eyes.

We nailed him to a Cross to be rid of him.
And still we build brick walls and concrete bunkers,
with manacles and statements and straitjackets to hold him,
but he, on the third day, walks out, leading
a little child by either hand.

The Spirit who is joy, and love, and gift,
nameless formless
rocking the sea;
breath of Eden
water of Jordan
newness of childhood
clear as flame;
gift of the two
who binds all together
girdle of love
in Jesus' name.

i. Alpha and Omega

Walk through Sion, walk all round it;
count the number of its towers.
Review all its ramparts,
examine its castles,

that you may tell the next generation
that such is our God.[1]

---

1. Ps 49 [48]:13-15.

Paradox

> I have learned that the place wherein Thou art found un-
> veiled is girt round with the coincidence of contradictories,
> and this is the wall of Paradise wherein Thou dost abide.[2]

A God beyond our grasping, who laughs at time and space.
The God of essence who translates himself into substance,
so that we may taste and see that he is good. The God who
explodes language and calls himself the Word. A God so great,
so alien, so other, that he takes into his lap the uncomforted
child that most of us remain lifelong, the weaned child that
rests more peacefully on its mother's breast than the burrow-
ing nursling, the infant unsteadily exploring the world, held
back from danger by the leading strings of love. The bridal
union is for grown-ups. Most of us never grow out of infancy,
stunted alike by ourselves and one another.

◆ ◈ ◆

We have lost the sense of paradox, which is why our the-
ology has long been fractured. All theology, all life is paradox.
Paradox is our window onto glory, our only language for it, a
God-given language.

◆ ◈ ◆

Since the late Middle Ages we see the Crucifixion as awful,
rather than aweful, but the Fathers saw it as the triumph of

---

2. Nicholas of Cusa, *The Vision of God*, trans. Emma Gurney Salter (New
York: Cosimo Classics, 2007), 44, chap. 9.

love, the triumph that trumped those of Caesar. The Resurrection was the evidence supplied for the weaker-minded, those who cannot see or understand.

Christ the king of love wears his crown on the Cross, an artefact woven by soldiers who, paradox to crown all paradoxes, in hailing him as king spoke the truth they were busily mocking and denying.

◆ ❖ ◆

The Word of God is defined for us in the richness of metaphor and the starkness of negation, but in the latter often walks unrecognized. We meet him there in paradoxical form, and in places well beyond the precincts of theology. My wandering mind was arrested recently by a few words of Samuel Beckett:

The sun shone, having no alternative, on the nothing new.[3]

This, I thought, is apophatic theology, and Beckett himself holds that door ajar by pointing us to Ecclesiastes: "There is nothing new under the sun."[4] But he is a writer who pursues the negative to the point where it opens onto infinity, the non-place without closure, and, led by this urgency, he sought continually to pare down his work, "stripping reality to its naked bones."[5]

---

3. Opening line of Beckett's first novel, *Murphy* (New York: Routledge, 1934).

4. Eccl 1:9.

5. Martin J. Esslin, "Samuel Beckett," *Encyclopedia Britannica* online. See also John Fletcher, *Beckett's Debt to Dante* (Edinburgh: Edinburgh University Press, 1965); www.eupublishing.com/doi/pdfplus/10.336/nfs.1965.005.

The author of Ecclesiastes, also notoriously negative, is given the lie in the penultimate chapter of the Book of Revelation, where God reveals himself as the great creator and perpetual renewer ("Behold, I make all things new").[6] Beckett's sentence points two ways, like all paradox, alternately true or false according to the context. It holds up a mirror image of truth and is, in its refinement, its true elegance, a reflection of the beauty of God.

6. Rev 21:5.

Truth

Truth so often—always?—faces two ways, Janus-like. This paradoxical element is its stamp of authenticity. We should look for it.

Truth: utter simplicity generating inexhaustible variety.

Truth is always subversive, which is why all establishment resists it. We will be judged on the persistence and passion with which we have questioned established wisdom, particularly the versions closest to our hearts and pockets.

"It is not Christ who is too good to be true; it is we who are not good enough to be true."[7]

"Our call is to a more naked faith and a more hopeless hope."[8] More Alice-in-Wonderland truths. We should all walk around on our heads; then we might see straight.

---

7. See Denys Turner, *Thomas Aquinas: A Portrait* (New Haven: Yale University Press, 2013), 222.

8. Michael Casey, "Bernard's Biblical Mysticism," *Studies in Spirituality* 4 (1994): 21, quoted in Maggie Ross, *Silence, A User's Guide, I* (Eugene, OR: Cascade Books, 2014), 171.

◆ ◈ ◆

In regard to the complex structures of the so-called real, including myself, I understand less and less. Alone shines clear the Incomprehensible; clear because utterly simple. I have looked on it as a brightness at the end of a telescope-like tunnel, the NO THING beyond things that is the object and fulfillment of all desire.

◆ ◈ ◆

Nowadays I believe only in the impossible.

◆ ◈ ◆

The truth is such a noble thing that if God were able to turn away from truth, I would cling to truth and let God go; for God is truth, and all that is in time . . . is not truth.[9]

---

9. Meister Eckhart, Sermon 11, *The Complete Mystical Works of Meister Eckhart*, ed. and trans. Maurice O'C. Walshe, rev. Bernard McGinn (New York: The Crossroad Publishing Company, 2009), 95.

Time and Eternity

We need to redefine our vocabulary: never-ending is not the
same as eternal.

The present moment offers a squint onto eternity, but we
prefer the rooms we have built to house past and future,
windowless but frescoed.

Eternity is not length of time, it is time telescoped out of
existence. It is the vanishing point of time. While we are still
in time, our meaning is in the waiting.

In the mathematics of eternity $(- = +)$. When all has been
given away the sum will be complete.

It is possible that the Last Judgment has already taken place.[10]

The cross is the form, the pattern, and the meaning. Time is
stretched out on the cross-piece where Christ's extended arms
reach from Paradise lost to Paradise regained. At the center, at
the intersection of time and eternity, is the riven heart of Jesus;
and each and all of us, wherever we are placed on history's
cross-bar, find ourselves also at that mystical intersection where

10. "It is already done" (Rev 21:6).

eternity is open to us in the present moment and we see the angels of God ascending and descending on the Son of Man.

Timeless, you operate in ways that make nonsense of our mental calendars and calculations. You are the apparently random, the inexplicable we call coincidence. You take some moment over which we think we have control, and like a conjuror you stick it up your sleeve and with sleight of hand pull out silk scarves of all the colors of the rainbow.

Trinity

I know now why the Father begot the Son: Love constrained him; Love begets love, it is Love's own law.

Indeed, if God is love, it follows that he is Three in One. For Love needs a Beloved, is incomplete without. The Spirit proceeds from the Two, for if two is fullness of a sort (an incomplete completion), three is balance, where stillness and movement become one. This One alone is adorable.

Paradox is at the heart of the Trinity, our God who is Three-in-One. We tend to prefer the word *mystery*, as being more encompassing, stretching farther, going deeper. There is pleasure in getting lost. Yet it can't easily escape the mutter of "cop-out, cop-out" rising from the pews. The harder-edged paradox is more exciting, a vertiginous word, and surely it is dizzying to ask his Mercy to plead in Person for us, to and against his Justice—God versus God?

Love of Nothing

This love has nothing in its sights
and aims so true
that out of everything there is
nothing will do.

And should love call by any name
(save only one)
the lover lost the lover found
nothing will come.

And yet one name to nothing is
the certain door
where love may enter knowing that
nothing is sure.

Knowledge and Meaning

Meaning is knowledge made active.

On Calvary knowledge was lodged only with the Father. Prophetic knowledge was given to the Son during his public life, as well as that which came from a relationship with the Father unclouded by sin. That knowledge was withdrawn during the Passion and hidden in the Father.

Meaning was embodied in the Son and given life through obedience, suffering, and love. Obedience is passive will, love is active will, and both were expressed in bodily suffering on the Cross: that was how the meaning was written out for us.[11]

Obedience was expressed in silence, love in the seven last words.

Knowledge was restored when Christ returned to the Father, and was given to us, in human measure and proportionate to our humility and longing, after the coming of the Spirit at Pentecost.

---

11. Obedience here is understood as the willed endurance that accepts and welcomes the underside of doing—the being done to, the Passion longed for in the Upper Room, dreaded in Gethsemane, undergone in the Praetorium and on Calvary.

Good and Evil

i

Good and evil manifest themselves in alien guises. There are extremes of evil, hard to imagine, yet immediately recognizable. An extreme of goodness is properly inconceivable. The good cannot be extreme, except possibly in the concept of excess as God's norm.[12]

Evil, which may present itself as harmless, even commendable at the outset ("if waterboarding one terrorist can save a hundred lives . . ."), is a shape-changer—it even took on an industrialized form in the Shoah (we may see different and worse in the future). It is the capacity of evil to generate power from within, to grow exponentially, that renders it frightening. We walk away from the slug-like thing in the woodshed, only to find it elsewhere, turned into a balrog.

No approach to evil, even in the mind or imagination, is without danger. It has the propensities of a virus, and to avoid contagion we need to be always washing our minds in the Holy Spirit.

It is—I think—impossible to envisage goodness otherwise than as individual acts, most often small. This is not to deny that good intentions and principles may be written into the foundational stratum of institutions, but these intentions and principles have to be constantly practised in word, gesture, and act. They come alive only at the relational level; they have, unlike evil, no quasi-independent existence.

12. Denys Turner, *Aquinas*, 204.

Faithfulness is the essential oil in the workings of goodness. Without it, at the institutional level these workings will seize up in a moment and cease to be effectual.

Our hope—at once tiny and infinite—lies newborn in a stable, and, like every infant, utterly dependent: a baby that depends on us to learn and teach the lesson of his weakness—namely that no gesture of love or goodness is too small to be significant, since the least may, in its place and time, prove strong as death.

ii

Life and death are relatives.
Good and evil are absolutes.
Naturally we have persuaded ourselves that the reverse is true.

Evil is inherently weak and would die if we ceased to feed it. It cannot exist without the tributes we bring it: our hatred, anger, lust, lies—so many lives offered to the Minotaur.
If the world throws its heart into the abyss, the beast will eat it and, growing huge, emerge to wreak its will.

We are never an end in ourselves, merely a channel for good or evil. Genes supply our specificity; grace, or its reverse, infuses our meaning. Free will is the spring on the door that we alone open or shut.

◆ ◈ ◆

We forget this truth at our peril, yet forget it we do; here is a recent reiteration by Christian Bobin:

> Evil is never spectacular at the outset. Evil always starts in the nicest way, modestly, one might venture: humbly. It seeps into the prevalent climate like water under a door.

Nothing significant to begin with. Just a spot of damp. When the flood comes, it is too late. The auxiliaries of evil are the half-heartedness and common sense of decent people. It is always what are called decent people who open the door to the ultimate horror.[13]

We are decent people, aren't we? Let us beware.

13. Christian Bobin, *La plus que vive* (Paris: Gallimard, 1996), 92.

Faith

There are times when reason is properly laid aside because faith is a burning torch and takes one so much further. With faith I can travel what seems like an infinite distance, a there-and-back through the darkness, all in the blink of an eye.

This faith has nothing to do with the "I believe" of the Credo. I believe in the creed in the sense that I don't argue with its articles; they are what I believe in; they are my gift from the Church.

Faith is an instant knowledge granted to love. It bypasses reason, for which it has no use. Returning from the darkness it lights up creation, showing it bathed in uncreated light.

When Turner uses as the subheading of a chapter, "Excess as the divine norm: the 'logic' of the Incarnation,"[14] he has, by his own admission in the use of single quotation marks, bypassed logic. He has written a phrase I do not have to follow through a maze of connectivity, but a swinging paradox I can grasp from the trapeze of intuition, a truth I can delight in.

14. Turner, *Aquinas*, 204.

Hope

There is a hope different from that which springs eternal in the human breast. It is the hope that walks between faith and love and remains when the other hope, as it can, fails.

This hope is a state of weightlessness. It is first and foremost the hope that Christ's great redemptive act will be—in time or out of it—brought to its greater conclusion, when all shall be well and all shall be one in him. Without this hope the darkness would be overpowering.

It is the hope that helps to set love in order in us, lifting us to a place where the air is thinner and our hopes for others are purified of the sly elements of desire and self-regard. It spans the divine silence between intercession and response, is immune to disappointment, oblivious of hurt. These remain, but on a lower level; they crawl and threaten, but weightlessness maintains us in the thinner air so long as we don't look down at them.

This hope is the gift of the Beloved. As it comes, unlooked for and undeserved, so it may go—yet not go, lie dormant and yet present, less felt than known. It may indeed be taken away before the end to make more room for love, so that love, which is the greatest, may go out in flood to meet the all in all.

Justice and Mercy

The injustice of our just God.

Creation was unable to attain its purpose because of him who kept it so in a state of hope.[15]

I was silent, not opening my lips, because this was all your doing.[16]

One might call God to account for original sin: for creating humankind with an innate flaw, a propensity to sin, and then telling his imperfect creatures to be perfect. The difficulty would appear to be partially resolved in Saint Paul's assurance that grace will be always proportionate to temptation. Thus we can say that sin is inevitable because of our weakness, but never, on any given occasion, necessary. We can go further with Julian of Norwich, who held that sin was "behovely," an integral part of the divine narrative, the last chapter of which was hidden from us and would remain so until the end of time.[17]

Justice and mercy surely operate according to different laws, for when both are absolute each cancels the other out; they cannot occupy the same space. There can be no limits to God's mercy: it is co-extensive with him, the emanation of his love.

15. Rom 8:20.
16. Ps 38 [39]:9.
17. See Denys Turner, *Julian of Norwich, Theologian* (New Haven: Yale University Press, 2011), 41–51, 115–20.

Justice, I would suggest, is of a radically different nature: it is the face of love seen by the imperfect, love as perceived by anyone in a state of sin. Justice in the form of punishment is what we expect of God, which is why the Old Testament is so full of it, projecting onto God the feelings and behavior that would be ours were we God. Mercy is not a natural human emotion: it has to be explained, promised, exemplified, enlarged upon, learned. Standing in the presence of perfect love, we would be consumed, as by fire, if mercy did not step in to clothe us. At the end of time we shall be self-condemned; the saving is of God, and who would set bounds to it?

When at the last truth tears aside the veil and we raise our eyes to the face of Christ, it will be in the collision of his mercy and our shame that we shall know the searing pain of purgatory. But a heart long closed to giving will not be open to receiving: anyone too hardened to forgive ends up by being too hard to be forgiven.

It is we, not God, who limit the operation of his mercy.

True humility can properly claim everything in the name of Jesus. Such boundless trust in God's love and mercy elicits and receives a boundless response: this is God's nature, love cannot do otherwise, it rushes to fill an emptiness, a yearning. And yet God is never manipulated, never forced, because grace is ever previous. This, and this alone, is the divine dynamic, *l'amor che move il sole e l'altre stelle.*[18]

18. "The love that moves the sun and other stars": Dante, *Paradiso,* XXXIII.145.

To make the imperfect perfect,
It is enough to love it.[19]

◆ ❖ ◆

God is justice; but when we pray, justice turns into mercy; it
happens of necessity, like a chemical reaction; prayer has this
power; it is what is meant by taking the kingdom by force.
When we pray, the divine hands bleed. Only the incarnation
made this possible; all is circular, leading back to the still point.

◆ ❖ ◆

I Will Arise and Go Now

My Lord, my love, the King of Hearts,
The nothing that holds all in fee
the silence in the listening air
the dead weight skewered to a tree;

I will get up from where I was
and go where I have ever been
through bilge-water as clear as glass
to look on what I've never seen.

19. Kathleen Raine, *Living With Mystery, Poems 1987–91* (Ipswich, UK:
Golgonooza Press, 1992), 59.

Presence/Absence

I recognise God's intervention in life's intricate minutiae, see his finger in the impossible coincidences, pregnant with meaning. I can believe in it too at the level of the galaxies.

But in the median dimension, the interval we call history, everywhere between Eden and the New Jerusalem, I meet his Absence, his Silence, his Non-Being.

He is not in the earthquake, the fire, or the flood; the senate, the barracks, the stock exchange, or any place where history is made.

The only signs of him are in a stable and on a hilltop. There the Absence becomes soft skin and bleeding flesh; the Silence, an infant's wail, the last cry of a dying man; Non-Being, a garden tomb.

The vulnerability of God is broken and scattered piecemeal through time, across the world, and takes flesh, not in Us, but only and always in the Other.

Suffering, dying, he is raised to life in us by love.

He must have been at Auschwitz, because if he chose not to be, I would choose not to know him.

Only those who were there have the right to speak of these places, but I take as my witness the Jewish historian Otto Dov

Kulka, who was himself in Auschwitz as a twelve-year-old boy and many years later had this remarkable dream:

> And I saw—the terrible grief of God, who was there. All that time. In His image. At first I felt Him (only) as a kind of mysterious radiation of pain, flowing at me from the dark void in the unlit part of the cremation ovens. A radiation of insupportably intense pain, sharp and dull alike. Afterwards He began to take the shape of a kind of huge embryo, shrunk with pain, in a murkiness amid which flickered only a little of the light cast by the raging fire locked in the heavy iron ovens . . . in the form He took here He was alive, shrunken, hunched forward with searing pain, as in the twisted posture of Rodin's sculpture *The Thinker.*[20]

Christ died on Golgotha for sinners, but also as victim for their, for our victims. The terrible grief of God there and here does not *explain* the suffering of the innocent, nor that of creation waiting for redemption together with humankind:[21] the mystery remains, but it has gained a counterweight that, with the adjunct of hope, renders it somehow, some of the time, endurable.

If we are now his hands, then he is our hurt.

20. *Landscapes of the Metropolis of Death* (London: Allen Lane, 2013), 98.
21. Rom 8:19-21.

Judgment

Christ on the cross promising Paradise to the repentant thief in Luke's gospel, and Christ enthroned in Last Judgments, with unseeing eyes, between the narrow path to heaven and the yawning mouth of hell, represent the ultimate paradox, the one we constantly—both historically and individually—fail to hold in balance.

There is an alternative diptych where the Fall faces the Last Judgment, and this is more enlightening. It gives us two great parables, to be understood metaphorically. In the first, the whole of humanity is here resumed in Adam and Eve, all history in the tree of the knowledge of good and evil, with the snake wound inextricably through its branches, all choice in Eve's hand stretched out for the apple.

In the second parable, the human race, now fragmented into as many individuals as the painter can cram into the canvas, is shown facing the consequence of those choices, most of which, unsurprisingly, are represented as bad. The enthroned and eternal Christ is in, quite literally, another world. He has devolved judgment to the archangel. The gate of Paradise is about to be shut again, not this time on everybody, but on a large number, suggesting that the death on Calvary was not very efficacious—but then mankind has always been hooked on Judgment, particularly for others.

Already in the third century Origen presented the Eden story as metaphor, or myth. That many in the twenty-first continue to read it literally shows how hard we find it to distinguish between fact and meaning, settling for a universal category of "fact"—"faction" perhaps? We still find it impossible to visualize punishment in any but human terms, merely extending the maximum sentence from life to eternity—which, if the soul is immortal, is the same thing. Those who cannot bridge the gulf between eternal fire and a God of love renounce either the one or the other.

◆ ◈ ◆

I used to wonder why the Father had handed over judgment to the Son: punishment seemed a much more father-like trait, well documented throughout the Old Testament, as well as in life. Now I see that revelation as the hinge, the very crux of Scripture, the moment where everything tips the other way: there on the Cross hangs our judgment. His coming in glory will simply make that clear, and we shall know judgment and forgiveness as one single act, the act of our salvation. In accepting the judgment, in passing through the fire of self-recognition, we shall open ourselves to him as he is, which is mercy. Seeing ourselves as we are will be our first sight of truth, the necessary prelude to glory. Perhaps indeed all was accomplished once and for all on Calvary: sacrifice, glory, and judgment in one timeless moment, since Christ was glorified in the crucifixion. For us, trapped in time, salvation history is stretched out like the Bayeux tapestry, but there is surely a sense in which we are already saved, and if saved, then already judged. Even the Bayeux tapestry can be thought of as one continuous present, where every event takes place here and now in front of the beholder. Time is still more blown open by those paintings that show the events of the Gospel, from annunciation to ascension, as taking place simultaneously in a common landscape. Not a lack of sophistication, but a different take on time and eternity.

◆ ◈ ◆

The perspective of judgment and mercy can be pushed still further, to the point where the two, like the parallel lines of a railway track, meet on the horizon and become indistinguishable. If Christ is the incarnation of divine mercy, then damnation is our choice, the last act of free will, when we refuse the mercy we see in the eyes of the Redeemer.

Moving backwards, not in time but from something to nothing, stripping away the veils of illusion and seeking a nakedness to cover me, I find at last, and put on, the transparent "Lord have mercy on me, a sinner." But One comes and takes it off, and hands me "God is Love."

Atonement

Twice lately I have heard or read the theologically literate affirming that there is no acceptable explanation for the atonement. None, that is, that is consistent with the behavior we would expect from a God who is love. But perhaps what goes to the heart of love has to be pushed outside the realm of logic, beyond the horizon of intellectual understanding. Words cannot explain the relationship of the Creator to the Word: the names "Father" and "Son" remain approximations, or, as Saint Ephrem would have it, the true reality—it is we who have / are the approximations.[22] It may be that we have to leave it in the domain of myth and in the language of poetry. Every living thing lives off others in order to survive. Something dies daily to ensure that I live, and by violence: the knife is taken even to the cabbage. All things resist death, out of the deepest of their inbred instincts; every root clings to its patch of soil; God alone went willingly to this slaughter of the innocent, becoming bread for us, for whom the natural bread, which ensures for a time the body's life, is not enough. Only the eternal God can give eternal life, in this world or the next. And only because his death was gift, standing the most basic law of creation on its head, is it redemptive. We are called to live à rebours, back to front, to embody a folly, to proclaim a paradox: what has been done *can* be undone, in blood we are washed white.

---

22. The terms *father* and *son* when applied to human beings "are borrowed names that through grace have taught us / that there is a single True Father / and that He has a single True Son" ("Faith," 46:12), in Sebastian Brock, *The Luminous Eye: The Spiritual World Vision of Saint Ephrem the Syrian*, CS 124 (Kalamazoo, MI: Cistercian Publications, 1992), 64.

By blood we live, the hot, the cold
To ravage and redeem the world
There is no bloodless myth will hold.[23]

The author of the Letter to the Hebrews saw and explored this crux in terms of the first covenant, and in those terms the argument is persuasive. But there remains, deeper than plummet, a mystery beyond our understanding, and poetry alone can maintain meaning open ended.

◆ ◈ ◆

Feast of the Exaltation of the Cross:
> Had there been no cross . . . there would be no streams of immortality pouring from Christ's side, blood and water for the world's cleansing. The legal bond of our sin would not be cancelled, we should not have attained our freedom, we should not have enjoyed the fruit of the tree of life and the gates of paradise would not stand open.

These lovely words of Saint Andrew of Crete form part of the Office of Readings for today—lovely in all but the clause "the legal bond of our sin would not be cancelled."[24] I cannot believe that God defines himself or his actions in legal terms, or that this is how he saw the crucifixion of his Son. The lesson of the Cross is surely that God is not within or outside the law, he is Other, and therefore beyond any such conception, let alone constraint. Saint Paul proclaims boldly that we are now free of the Law, but in fact he has reintroduced it into the

---

23. Geoffrey Hill, "Genesis V," *Collected Poems* (New York: Penguin, 1985), 16.

24. The formula varies with the translation: the current rendering of "legal bond" in the Liturgy of the Hours is "record," but the concept remains pervasive and persistent.

equation in making that freedom a condition of our salvation: if this were so, Christ himself would be bound by a necessity.

But God introduced the Law on Sinaï, not out of *his* necessity, but ours, as a part of our education, like times x tables. And Christ freed us, not from a legal prescription, but from a natural law of consequence ("if you do bad things worse will automatically follow"). He freed us through forgiveness, which severed the tie, enabling repentance and *conversatio morum*. But we, being inherently legal minded, have never made this leap into the true, the utter freedom of forgiveness. Instead we have too often interpreted the Cross in legal terms, bordering on financial ("There was no other good enough / To pay the price of sin"). Metaphorical, perhaps, but such a narrow and constricting metaphor!

In love with Roman law, the Church introduced canon law, which, loved in turn, grew exponentially, while ironically, over against the growing legalism of the educated and clerical classes in the later Middle Ages; the essential (if often disregarded) words at the heart of the lay feudal bond were *love* and *service*.

Human laws are necessary to ensure justice in a human and often inhumane society, but the Church should be wary of giving the concept of Law free run in the house of Love and make sure that it gets walked and kennelled well away from Calvary.

Freedom and Foreknowledge

The one does not negate the other; it is only our inability to move out of our own context that lands us in such blasphemous nonsense as predestination to hell. We are only wholly safe when enclosed in the womb of God's perfect foreknowledge; only there are we already whole and entire, and that fact dispels all anxiety, for we can say with Christ, *consummatum est.* Yet that doesn't limit our freedom; it doesn't diminish it even fractionally, for the foreknowledge of God is so great as to embrace all possibilities, it is so limitless as to contain all our choices, it enfolds without constraining: such is our God.

Everything done to us, all happenings lie within God's foreknowledge, and by accepting in love we make these into his will for us. It lies within our power to force the Father's hand.

To be truly free we need to escape from the imprisonment of context. We often think we are choosing freedom when we are simply escaping from one context into another: the certainties of the Socialist Workers are just as confining as the complacencies of the *bien pensant.* All ideologies constrain, limit, bind, imprisoning and ultimately betraying the truths they contain. Insofar as we accept a context—social, ideological, religious even—without struggling constantly to escape from it, we are all figures of Epstein's Lazarus, wound in our grave-clothes. We have to go out—out of the city, out of the camp, to where the wind blows free on Golgotha. There is only one way out of a rule and that is inward—inward and down. There is nothing so radical as prayer.

Nothing is fixed except what is hidden in the mind of the Father.[25]

25. Matt 24:36; Mark 13:32.

Failure

Our spiritual life, which is our love life, cannot be other than a failure when measured against the Gospel, against Christ's challenge to be perfect. That is, if we define failure as the world defines it, the world being the culture that shapes us and determines our interpretations of experience. The concept of failure implies the existence and acceptance of certain norms, along with the expectation that we will attain them; this is made plain to us from infancy onwards. Yet perfection lies, almost by definition, beyond normal reach.

So where does that leave failure, if we use perfection as a touchstone?

The answer may well be: nowhere; for a concept depends on our ability to define it, and a change of cultural parameters can put a definition at risk. The noun *failure* does not seem to figure in Scripture. The verb is common enough with the sense of lack, want—the olive crop fails, the courage of the troops fails—there is not the sense of moral dereliction ("I am a failure") now attached to the word. In the Vulgate New Testament, the standard translation of the Middle Ages, the verb *deficere* is rare. Significantly, just before his passion the Lord prays for Peter, that his faith may not fail, shrivel like the olive crop—*ne deficiat fides tua*. Peter's faith did fail; even Christ's prayer was not enough, which sheds a singular light on the relationship between the Father and the incarnate Son. Jesus knew too that it wouldn't be answered in a literal sense, or not before the coming of the Spirit, for he goes on quietly to say *et tu aliquando conversus, confirma fratres tuos*.[26]

In one sense Peter's faith did fail: like a failed harvest, it fell short, dried up. In another sense it was a *felix culpa*: it was

26. Luke 22:32.

Peter's Golgotha, for in that failing, that death, fell to earth the wheat grain from which his resurrection life grew. Failure in the context of Scripture becomes indefinable. Since we cannot know the mind of God we cannot know the meaning of our lives, nor properly apportion success or failure, except when measured against narrow and very specific goals, and even in such cases we usually find that while our backs were turned, time, or God, has moved the posts. Failure, I suspect, does not even exist in the mind of God, since the word that goes out from his mouth never returns empty.[27]

Failure in the context of the spiritual life, that is of life *tout court*, has neither place nor meaning unless held within an all-encompassing mercy, a sea of mercy, an ocean of mercy. In which case our failures, real or supposed, become something to embrace.

The Gospel provides us with no definitions of the things that matter. Pilate was quite right in his own terms when saying, "What is truth?" He got no answer, and nor did Thomas, although he framed the question differently.[28] Or rather, Thomas got an answer, but no definition, because God is by nature indefinable. The great things are all indefinable. Maybe this is what W. S. Graham meant by the words, "And the great humilities, / Leave us always ill at ease."[29] Or maybe not; poets themselves do not always know the meaning of what they have written: meaning is manifold and meanings escape from poems like wriggling worms through the holes in a colander. God alone knows all his meanings.

27. Isa 55:11.
28. John 14:5.
29. W. S. Graham, "Hilton Abstract," in *Selected Poems* (London: Faber and Faber, 1996), 70.

◆ ◈ ◆

The etymology of failure and its French counterparts *défaut* (Eng *default*) and *échec*—which last, thanks to the medieval passion for chess, seems to have replaced Old French forms of Vulgar Latin *fallere*—all these words have, as original meaning, shortfall and also rift, non-connection, as in fault line.

◆ ◈ ◆

I sense a mysterious connection between failure and negativity. Both represent the underside of existence, the minus mode. It may be that neither has any real existence, just as it has been argued that evil does not exist.

◆ ◈ ◆

Prayer is no guarantor of success under any heading: we should learn to love our failures, that they too may find their place in the will of God.

ii. The Words We Use

If there only existed a single sense for the words of Scripture, then the first commentator who came along would discover it, and other hearers would experience neither the labour of searching, nor the joy of finding. Rather, each word of our Lord has its own form, and each form has its own members, and each member has its own character. Each individual understands according to his own capacity and interprets as it is granted him.

Saint Ephrem the Syrian[1]

---

1. "Commentary on the Diatesseron," 7–22, quoted in Sebastian Brock, *The Luminous Eye: The Spiritual World Vision of Saint Ephrem the Syrian*, CS 124 (Kalamazoo, MI: Cistercian Publications, 1992), 49.

Words

Conceived beyond bounds of language
Born of the uttered *fiat*
All emanations of the Word
Shout in the interstellar silence.

The elemental substances
Supply the phonemes,
The complex filigrane of species
The celestial accidence
Without irregularity;
Each creature in its quiddity
Proclaims itself, a nonce-word,
Echoing its singularity
In the eternal mind.

We are the verbs:
Past, present and conditional,
Active and passive,
Syntactical necessities
Fusing the undirected clamor
Into a hymn of praise
Or scream of pain.
All other forms are fixed,
We only are empowered to choose
Our verbal incarnations,
And by semantic metamorphosis
To change our meaning,
As snakes will slough their skins
Time and again.

And this the sin:
To wrest creation's language
And misconstrue its sense
Till given rules are disremembered
And usage lost
That will not be relearned,
Nor harmony restored,
Until the creative *fiat*
Freely conferring freedom
Meets in each act the willed response
Fiat voluntas tua.

The God of Words and Silence

i

Good children used to be seen and not heard. With the God of Abraham, Isaac, and Jacob the reverse was the case. Scripture rings with the yearning wail, "When shall I enter and see the face of God?" The answer was daunting: "You cannot see my face, for one can see me and live." Even Moses was granted no more than a glimpse of the Lord's back. This God, on the other hand, is rarely silent. From Genesis to Zechariah he is teaching, scolding, soothing, wheedling, pleading with his people. He speaks to Adam in the garden, to Moses on the mountain, to Job on his dunghill; he speaks in the thundercloud and the whispering breeze, he speaks interminably through the prophets, he even makes jokes, though his interlocutors don't always think them funny. So garrulous is he that when he falls silent his people get worried: he doesn't love us any more, they wail.

The God who finally revealed himself as Trinity is a God who communicates: it is part of the divine nature. Where human beings are concerned, the God of love is also the God of language, but just as in our communication with him we see mostly with the mind's eye, so we hear mainly with the ear of the heart.

This God, being God, is inexpressible; all language stumbles and fails; there is a sense in which we are mute before him. So we turn to his creation for word pictures and figures of speech that help us to creep closer, and in doing so, according to Saint Ephrem, the best loved of the Syriac Fathers, we are only copying God himself who set the example, dressing himself in metaphors familiar to us, so that we might better recognize and understand him: "It is our metaphors that He put on; though He did not literally do so. . . . He puts one on when it is beneficial, then strips it off in exchange for another."[2] And in so doing he has given us permission to do likewise and fashion a language in which we can speak with and about God: the language he—or his interpreters—used in Scripture, the language of the Fathers, but which since the rise of Scholasticism and the advent of the Enlightenment has been elbowed aside as being for the less sophisticated.

ii

The unknowable, indefinable God has defined himself in the Word: he is the Father's meaning.

You, incarnate Christ, are become the careful grammar of our worship, the freer syntax of our mutual service; you are the true language of our minds and hearts, the unknown language of the silence whose utterance you are and which we shall articulate at the last.

The first Pentecost was a reversal of Babel. The Spirit manifested itself as a linguistic babble where each language was yet perfectly heard, perfectly understood. In Time we were shown the language of Eternity, our own made new, healed and restored to purpose.

There are senses in which God is our vernacular:

2. Brock, *Luminous Eye*, 60–61.

He is the breath in our nostrils.

In the Hebrew Scriptures he presents himself alternately as father, mother, spouse.

> In the crib at Bethlehem he takes on our dailiness, our ordinary, the vernacular of our lives.

◆ ◈ ◆

Christ is for ever strung between Babel and Pentecost. Were we aware of this, we would give language the care and honor it deserves. When we give words their full weight of meaning, cradling it consciously and lovingly, feeling the tug of gravity, we are helping to support the weight of his body. The crucified is the true signifier, extending his meaning to all creation.

◆ ◈ ◆

The Father yielded his Word into the hands of the translators: it was the first incarnation and also the source of the first betrayal, the Word being of its nature inexpressible. But like Peter's it has proved a *felix culpa,* as was of course foreseen.

◆ ◈ ◆

Prophets alone know the unlearnt language of the Word; they are its true translators, drawing meaning down for us in words of light.

◆ ◈ ◆

We were given religious language to express those truths that our cultures persistently deny. Once—when we had the script sufficiently by heart for some at least to follow it—it came dressed in flesh and was acted out before us, the first Mystery Play.

On Being Translated—A Fairy Tale

During his years as a Benedictine abbot, before his move in 1135 to the Cistercians at Signy, William of Saint-Thierry wrote down his thoughts—the subject of much reading and more prayer—entitled them *Meditationes,* and shared them with his Carthusian friends at Mont-Dieu. He wrote them of course in Latin.

Eight and a half centuries later, these thoughts, in English now, were flown high over continents to a small island in the China Seas where they were read to a community of Cistercian monks, who had no Latin, whose mother tongue was Cantonese, but who knew just enough English to look through its frosted glass into William's mind. What they found there so delighted them that their abbot sought permission to translate the precious writings into Cantonese.[3] As William's mind, when he wrote his *Meditations,* was filled with God, the three languages linked hands to transfer God on the magic carpet of technology across time and space. And naturally, on arrival, he was instantly recognized and honored.

3. My thanks to Brian Patrick McGuire, the visiting lecturer who read to the community from *The Cistercian World* and contacted me afterwards by email.

Adventures of Mistranslation

It can happen that passages from the Fathers move me so powerfully that I close the book and push it away, fearing to be overwhelmed. Last night the phrase *opprimetur a gloria* came swimming up like a tadpole through the pool of memory, and this morning I took down a Concordance and found Proverbs 25:27, rendered in the Douai version as "he that is a searcher of majesty shall be overwhelmed by glory." But not in the modern translations: New Jerusalem, faithful to the Hebrew author, reduces the passage to a banal warning against self-flattery or fishing for compliments. Thank God for Jerome, who struck from false science so brightly minted a phrase, one that sparkles out like a diamond down the centuries from page after page of sober Latin commentaries, a phrase that became a proverb in its own right, enabling generations of old men to snub enquiring minds. Glory be to the Spirit who brings such gems from mistranslation, improving, dare one say, on his own original. These too are among God's "dappled things," the multi-faceted and multi-layered, those with many meanings, where nothing is quite what it seems.

Ten years on, I should like to add a further paean to the felicities of mistranslation, and to the Holy Spirit, who brings truth out of error in such serendipitous ways. Again Jerome stands alone on his hill with a phalanx of post-sixteenth-century translators ranged in the plain against him. The verse in contention is Song of Songs 2:4, which in the Vulgate reads *Ordinavit in me caritatem*. English translations from the Hebrew have, "And his banner over me was love," a metaphor of great beauty: a banner, held high, is a sign of both authority and protection. Here it floats free in the wind of the Spirit and the only authority it claims is that of love. It is at once a declaration and an invitation.

Jerome's version, rendered in English as "He has set love in order in me,"[4] must be one of the most commented verses in Scripture, and for good reason, for it is theologically richer than the other. Our lives, from birth to death, are meant to be an education in reforming our self-love and winkling it out from the other loves it preys on parasitically and distorts. We need both versions, the "correct" and the "incorrect." The latter—Jerome's understanding—is the one we are given to work with through the heat of the day; the modern scholars' version is the one for resting in when evening comes.

God is patient and allows us time to revisit our own imperfect understandings. I now see the shut-the-book phrases that threaten to overwhelm me as being precisely those that are infused with a glimpse of his glory. They carry, too, the warning that issued from the burning bush on Mount Horeb: *"the place where you are standing is holy ground."*[5] Moses was told to stay where he was and take off his sandals. Barefoot he stands before God, mantled in awe—the fear of God which made the prophets quake and which we have replaced with an easy familiarity (and we know what *that* can breed). When we brush up against that alien awe in a shut-the-book moment, we back off, not so much overwhelmed by glory as scared of what this God might want of us. His mere proximity threatens to burst the limits of our clichéd view of him. What might not follow? How much easier to tiptoe away flattering oneself on one's "sensitivity."

---

4. Douai version: "He set charity in order in me."
5. Exod 3:3.

Language and Liturgy

The language spoken at the Last Supper was almost certainly Aramaic. In what language did the Apostolic Church continue to break bread? Would a certain discomfort have been felt in using Hebrew, the ancestral language of worship? What language did Saint Paul pray in once he got to Damascus, and in Arabia? Most of these men had three languages at their disposition, and Latin will not have been one. As for the centurion who taught innumerable Christians to repeat in his wake, "Lord, I am not worthy that you should enter under my roof, but only say the word . . . ," in what language did he utter the words attributed? Had he been in the country long enough to learn the local vernacular, or did he use *koine* Greek, assuming that Jesus and his disciples would understand it? The one certainty is that Christianity was from the start multilingual, Pentecost at once symbolic and prophetic.

Yet we have always undervalued our vernaculars, investing Latin with an intrinsic value that no language can properly lay claim to. There is nothing fixed about language, languages are born and grow; they morph into others; many eventually die, some linger on as ghosts. All change can feel threatening, and language, being an important constituent of identity, has this potential to a high degree. The young are the drivers of change: the latest slang, the newest buzz-words put them in the vanguard where they long to be. Their grandparents carry banners for the grammatical norms they grew up with; they often have a point, but they always lose. The use of any language in liturgy puts a brake on this normal process of evolution, and sooner or later there comes a conflict between progress and evolution, clarity and nostalgia, which is rarely altogether amicable.

Latin has been no one's mother tongue for many centuries. Its place in the Church and more particularly in the liturgy has been hallowed by time, and it is right that it should be; right too that Latin should be held most precious where it has been most used, as in monastic chant. It would be a matter of deep sadness were it to vanish from the liturgy, and a crime if it were banished, which of course is inconceivable. But Latin is not *better than* the vernacular, just *different from*. The *best* language, or at least the most fitting [*justus*] for the liturgy is the one that allows us all to worship the Father in spirit and in truth. And who shall decide what that is except the Spirit in the Church?

Moreover, every language has what the French term *son génie*, its distinctive nature, and none should be translated without great sensitivity on the part of the translator to the need for preserving this. Linguistic mongrels have few beauties, and English crossed with Latin is a graceless cur.

Trouble with Adjectives

There is something unfortunate about the adjectives we hang
round the neck of the Church: *militant* and *triumphant* never
had much to recommend them and should be, if not con-
signed to history, left to the Latin Mass Society for its nostalgia
cupboard. A more recent word, *institutional*, is even worse:
nobody loves an institution (though perhaps we should). And
alas, of the popular definition of institutions as self-serving,
sclerotic, probably corrupt, chiefly intent on their own pres-
ervation, the Church has latterly shown itself the perfect example. To the joy of its foes and the grief of its members it
has assumed an identity that is utterly loathsome: *whore of
Babylon* had a certain cachet, *institutional* has none. Nor can
the Church be represented as an Aunt Sally, unjustly bom-
barded with coconuts by a hostile crowd, a victim role put
forward by a substantial section of its hierarchy. Sadly, in its
present state it is stuck with this adjective, and worse ones
too, just as we, its members, are stuck with the Church. So
how can we continue to love and support it?

For a start it is still the Church of the poor and the mar-
tyrs, the exploited and the persecuted throughout the world.
It is also the Church of the saints, both recognized and others unknown except to those whom they serve. And if we
look back to Acts and the letters of Saint Paul, it is plain that
the apostolic church—clearly not yet institutional in the full
sense—was already incipiently so, arguing within its own parameters over a range of problems touching faith and morals:
the institution was starting to emerge, as it had to; no human
grouping can survive without a framework and regulations to
define its purpose and behavior. The fractiousness of Paul's
churches, which caused him so much pain, was part of a pro-

cess. Much more significant is the founding principle on which he established these bodies politic: not a set of rules but a living metaphor, the body of Christ, a body wounded, crucified, but also resurrected. This is their true reality, and as such it is about life and growth, about change within one unchanging and integrated whole. Moreover, that life—the life of the body whose head is the Christ who "makes all things new"—should be a daily process of reform from within, a process that might see the hierarchy fasting and the laity praying for them rather than the reverse as was recently suggested, and all united in the humility that, for Saint Benedict, was the doorkeeper to life in Christ. Paul at times criticized the churches he had founded; he also prayed for them continuously. Criticism alone will not bring about root and branch reform; we need to study Hosea to find our way back to loving the Church, ourselves included.

Pack of Lies

These words aren't mine, I do not
Own them. They are a pack
Of curs I keep to fetch
And hunt and tell my love.

Ill-bred for the most part, they
Slink in at nightfall, untrained
And graceless. Feeling at home
They settle in, to whelp

In corners. Barking, biting,
Baying to the moon is all
Their art, lifting forlorn muzzles
They are yet out of tune.

My one good bitch is Silence;
Coarse of coat, silken-eared,
In the thorn thickets hers
The sole voice ringing true.

Words

i

My own way of expressing myself almost always disappoints
me. I am anxious for the best possible, as I feel it in me
before I start bringing it into the open in plain words: and
when I see that it is less impressive than I had felt it to be,
I am saddened that my tongue cannot live up to my heart.[6]

---

6. Augustine, *On Catechising Beginners* ii, 3, quoted in Peter Brown,
Augustine of Hippo: A Biography (Berkeley: University of California Press,
1969), 256.

Thus Augustine the preacher. And so, too, each one of us: poet, writer, musician, painter, and, indeed, comforter, parent, friend. Yes, words are for ever failing us—deserting us, refusing to come together and form the clear, the necessary links leading back to our fugitive experiences of truth. Worse, they betray us, welling up like bilge-water from flooded drains. We open our mouths and they fall out, graceless, squalid, malevolent, loaded. They run around, combining in ways we hardly recognize—yet do, for if we are honest there is no denying their breeding.

ii

Embroidering facts is frowned on—or used to be—on the ground that a fact is a plain Jane and what you see is what you get. One can conceive, though, of facts so stupendous that those who witness them and reflect on them might wish to pick them out in gold thread in order to bring out their intrinsic beauty. Embroidery can also trace, suggest, or supply hidden meaning. In the case of the infancy narratives, the prophets, and particularly Isaiah, were plundered for gold thread. Saint Luke knew where to look and was an artist with the needle—what would we have done without him?

Prophecy: foresight and hindsight so dovetailed that the process can be read from either end—forwards by the believer, backwards by the sceptic—ensuring that freedom is always safeguarded, faith never constrained.

iii

We like our motives baroque, even self-indulgently rococo, but God is supremely simple, and thus the ultimate in elegance.

iv

I once heard it said that *should, must,* and *ought to* were not God words. *More,* said the speaker, was a God word. I had never seen the oyster of the human psyche prized open in so neat and economical a way. I felt myself instantly exposed, and what lay within was so poor a thing: a lifetime's choice of shriveled words, used to keep Christ at bay.

v

The newest forms of technology offer equivalences for the oldest insights, emphasizing the oneness of indwelling truth throughout creation. The smart card serves as an analogy for faith, passing through barriers, opening doors. Faith is our proximity card to Christ in the tabernacle, to the essence in the accidents; we hold it up, it decodes the mystery, and we pass in.

vi

Snuggle, as a word, is hard to rival for marriage of sound and sense. *Cuddle* tries but is hampered by its hard consonants; only its ending keeps it in the race and out of the cowshed. *Snuggle* is inviting: come in and try it, it says. Puppies snuggle adorably, foals and lambs have difficulties with legs: they wobble more convincingly. *Snuggle*, I think, implies a wish for company, though a big, soft blanket will suffice. In puppies it has a close cousinage with *snuffle* (in people this is better avoided). Snuggling is impossible on a board or hurdle and was not practised by the Desert Fathers or hermits of any cloth or none. It was however granted a Benedictine passport of sorts by Dom Henry Wansborough, who once affirmed that Lent was a time for snuggling up to God.

vii

Words never cease to surprise us, since, fortunately, we never cease to learn. There floated into my mind the other day the phrase "We may not know, we cannot tell," first heard as a child in the hymn, "There is a green hill far away." I absorbed knowing and telling instinctively as two ways of saying the same thing. Scripture is full of such doublets, and common speech confirmed this understanding, where phrases like "You can never tell," and "There's no telling," served merely to underline the frontier between known and unknown. This morning I suddenly understood knowing and telling as a progression. We can indeed not tell what we don't know, and telling has significance in the passing on of knowledge, essential to the survival of individual and community.

Learn, understand, know, love, tell. To know God is to love him, and to love is to know. Knowing and loving are fulfilled in telling—a trinitarian relationship where the third proceeds from the two. And also the essence of the Gospel: Christ gave his disciples knowledge, loved them to the end, bade them tell the whole world.

viii

Words have a trinitarian instinct, they like to go in threes: Father, Son, and Spirit; the Way, the Truth, and the Life; faith, hope, and charity. The poet Péguy saw faith, hope, and charity as three little girls skipping along, holding hands. All are mysteriously interrelated. Saint Paul's three, much oftener quoted than the second set, look strangely lower case beside the others, and not just for want of capitalization—more as though they were for us and not for God. In his first letter Saint John pipes up like a blackbird, linking the first and last set: *Deus caritas est* (one truth in three words)—not *amor*, not *eros*: God—and God alone—is himself *caritas*, the perfect, the self-giving love. In him all loves are subsumed in one; meanwhile we, who are so good at misusing the others, wait on grace for the gift of this.

ix

The devil is out of fashion (except among the literal-minded). But just as he appeared written off, he found strange new verbal life in *demonize*. Demonizing is a popular sport that encourages the multiplication of different forms of pseudo-devil, which can be controlled and kept out of the house. The prototype meanwhile is back indoors, where he always was, without benefit of name or shape, a miasma, feeding on our detritus, ultimately on us.

x

Language may default on me before the end, and might be the hardest betrayal my body has up its sleeve. With *may* and *might* I am happy to say that I still have a good understanding.

xi

The words on a computer screen are normally black on white. Sometimes, when we run our cursor over the text, a word turns blue, as though it became alive and was offering to lead us somewhere else, to another context, another country.

The same thing can be true of words on a page, those that have some special link to truth; they can turn blue, individually, or more often in a phrase. This energy comes from the relation between our words and the Word—and this itself is a mystery inviting deeper study. The propensity of words to turn blue is greatest in Scripture. Theologians are not necessarily favored; this is sad, since they should, as the servants of truth, use only words that have the qualities of stained glass and that, when assembled, spell out God's greatness, his mercy, or his glory.

When words turn blue in this way it is a gift, to the writer first who facilitated the process by keeping out of the way and by providing, like a good jeweler, the right setting. Above all to the reader who sees the blue, pauses, and follows to the open country where it leads.

Turning words blue is the work of the Spirit, the Spirit that proceeds from the Word.

The French prose poet Christian Bobin, who spurns the computer and thus the Internet, is none the less versed in the virtues of blue, beginning one of his books, "Let's start with this blue if you will. The blue of a freshened April morning. . . . I should like to write you a letter composed only of this blue."

It ends thus: "I look at the sky's blue. There's no door there. Or if there is it has been open all along. . . . This blue, I'm slipping it into this book, for you."[7]

Whatever comes out of the blue should be given a welcome—it might be an angel in shirtsleeves.

7. *The Eighth Day, Selected Writings of Christian Bobin*, chosen and translated by Pauline Matarasso (London: Darton, Longman & Todd, 2015), 179, 204.

Mood Change

We should not say, "I have changed," but "I have been changed,"
since all change for good originates with the Father of lights,
and only the passive form properly conveys our relationship
with a God who is initiator, guide, and end. Yet so sold are we
on doing, seeking meaning in a ceaseless whirl of activity to
fend off boredom (death being boredom made permanent) that
we are constantly inventing active usages for verbs that were
only used in the passive a generation ago. Where our parents
were converted, by preaching or example or the Holy Spirit,
we now "convert"—ourselves, rarely others—autonomous,
self-motivated, the captains of our souls.

In what sense can we be said to do God's will if he, as Julian
of Norwich understood it, is the only doer?[8] The most we
can desire and pray for is to be so disposed that he is able to
work his will in us: we clothe ourselves in the Passive Voice,
in which he calls us to be active. This is not a form of quiet-
ism, a sitting waiting for guidance. It is using confidently the
gifts we have been given, reading the signs, while trusting that
the pattern will emerge and that the word spoken, usually in
silence, will not return empty. It seems to me that the saints
who take the kingdom of God by force proceed more often
than not like this. Being better listeners, they hear the word
more clearly and venture more boldly, and the Spirit hastens
to give the kaleidoscope a new and glorious twist.

8. Julian of Norwich, *A Revelation of Love*, ed. Marian Glasscoe (Exeter:
University of Exeter Press, 1986), 17–18, §11.

◆ ◈ ◆

Christ as Word, Logos, Verbum, the working word, active, through whom all things were made. Yet when he came to earth he was not doer but done to. God *made* flesh, God *nailed* to a cross, God *raised* from the dead. God in the passive, obedient unto death.

Now we represent him as risen, triumphant. Yet in this long interim of post-Resurrection time I see him with his hands still tied, just as when he stood before Pilate or submitted to being the plaything of the soldiers. He has handed all activity to the Spirit, and, with his words to Peter, "feed my sheep," to us, that is to the saints among, or—who knows?—within us: our better selves.

Telling Stories

i

We are inveterate tellers of tales. We tell ourselves over and over the stories of our lives, past, present, and future, fashioning out of the debris of events and experience a pseudo-reality, explaining our selves to ourselves, creating the acceptable image, the one we can open the door to. These narratives offer a varying mixture of self-understanding and self-deception, and always with self-justification as the rarely acknowledged motive. My fictions fill my head with their rubbish. Their refrains are set to discordant jingles, which reverberate round the echo chambers of my skull till all is disjointed, set at odds, teeth-on-edge, screeching. For all our stories have a back door ajar onto chaos, impossible to force shut. He/we alone can guard it: he alone in his pre-emptive grace, we alone in the will's vigilance; we, unsleeping in his strength, he, ever watchful in our weakness; we in that weakness crying "Jesus!"—he sending his angel to stand guard in our stead.

Yet God, the sole author of our world and every other, is the only true spinner of yarns since he alone holds the thread of our meaning. He, Truth, is the teller, and he, Word, the tale, the one we ought to be reading and rereading, the one that is always new, whose language we learn, childlike, as we turn the pages, the one that has a resolution but no ending. It is the story Mary was listening to while Martha muttered "It's not fair," the tale that quietens the head and quickens the heart, and as we read we should be copying it out for him in loving service and in poverty of spirit.

ii

The saints have revelations—the direct illumination that may still require the interpretation that turns it from visual, and therefore instant, into narrative. It took Julian of Norwich twenty years to produce the Long Text. The rest of us are given anecdotes, in the form of happenings that erupt into what we think of as the normal course of life, to be picked up or not, understood or not, according to the mysterious interaction of free will and grace. This should be no surprise since most of Scripture is a narrative. Unlike the narratives we write ourselves, the anecdotes we are given are always unexpected and usually subversive. This is their warranty. There is often a comic element, for God is not merely the God of surprises, but also the God of jokes, who invites us to laugh at ourselves. These anecdotes come often in installments, and we find them linking themselves into strands of our lives that increase their authority. When a message comes flagged up in this way, it would be foolish to ignore it. Such messages have the potential to turn one's life inside out.

iii

Tale Telling

I am a story walking, line
by line; a tale with layers
of non-meaning and
more than one author;
for anyone interested but chiefly
for myself
I supply an interlinear gloss
revised and updated daily.
We are a narrative species, a
collective roman fleuve
whose God (some say)
made himself linear and spanned
the alphabet
reserving thus to himself the best
story and leaving for Satan
only the tunes.

Maker, walker, and tale
of me are one; I
haunt the margins—prosy, self-mocking,
vaporing, smug, lewd; those
who can't read their text
doodle till time is squeezed
to death, and meaning
springs clear.

iv

All art is a bringing to birth. It is not a matter of creating
out of nothing but of liberating what is already there, in the
strict sense a labor. The sculptor frees the form concealed in
the stone. The analogy is plain since the stone, the material,
is already visible, gravid with a weight it is destined to lose,
yielding it reluctantly into the hands of the artist. The poem is
no less brought to birth, eased out of chaos where all meanings
pre-exist—incipient, mingled. Words are the tools that give
these meanings their shape and ease them into being, and in
so doing the words become the poem, the form in which the
meaning is embodied. The poet is at once midwife and maker.
There is a hidden kernel in a poem that is gift, for words as
tools, however consciously picked and placed, play their own
part in shaping the meaning, so that the poet, like the midwife,
bends at the end to receive and greet a child unknown in its
particularity. There is often an element of surprise in seeing
one's child—or one's poem—for the first time: intimately
known, it is nonetheless its own person.

Why, What, How

Evelyn Waugh combined a few banal words and gave them to
Sebastian Flyte, in whose mouth they took wing: challenged
to defend his belief in the Christmas story, he does so on the
grounds that "it's a lovely idea." "But you can't believe things
because they're a lovely idea," replies his friend. "But I do.
That's how I believe."[9] There is more here than an appeal to
aestheticism. The "how" is different from the "why" and the
"what." It is saying that religion is more than a creed, that the
divine cannot be summed up in formulae, that analogy opens
a different sequence of doors.

The "how" is also, in a strange yet profound sense, domestic. Belief is a lonely thing. It is a human being standing
on a promontory looking out to sea. The Church tried for a
time to furnish it with community credentials by starting the
Creed with the firm declaration: *We believe*. It was a good
try, but we remained pews of individuals standing shoulder to
shoulder, each professing an individual belief, with or without
reservations, in a series of dogmas.

Faith is different; it is a participation in a unique narrative, through listening, rehearsing, and even by contributing to
the next chapter. The other stories that we tell ourselves are
invariably autobiographical, spun out of our own experience,
but faith offers for our exploration a compendium of tales already densely populated, in which the parts we play are pretty
unimportant; in fact the more frequently we visit that country,
the more insignificant our entrances and exits appear. And yet
these faith stories are essentially welcoming and inclusive, even

9. Evelyn Waugh, *Brideshead Revisited* (London: Everyman's Library,
1993), 76.

allowing for our participation as co-authors—within limits: we can enter into Gospel situations, we can invite the saints into our living-rooms; what we cannot do is direct the conversation. In different degrees, and in ways that escape easy definition, many of the faithful live in a quasi-domestic familiarity, sometimes with Our Lord, often with the Virgin and the saints, in a relationship that has little to do with belief as usually understood—it is rather an extension of life.

It is good to make public profession of the truths enshrined in the Creed. But the emphasis since the Enlightenment on reason as the only foundation for belief, and latterly on the biological sciences, seen as underlying all intellectual activity—and indeed psychological and even spiritual insofar as the last is allowed to exist—has left other approaches to truth without either legitimacy or verisimilitude. The parallel dominance of Aristotelian logic in theology since the Scholastics has also been damaging. Living in faith takes place in another dimension, which has been largely overlooked and often undervalued. One believes in a truth, one has faith in a person. It happens, when that Person is Truth, and only then, that the dimensions become fused. Meanwhile my unknown self feeds on grace, moves in how, perceives in blue; I am not sure that it believes at all.

Monastic Office

All the beauty of the Psalms is of God; the anger and the violence are ours; we offer both with Christ, since the sacrifice of praise and the sin offering are now made one in him.

To God, with others, for others.

Careful attention threading the frayed strands of experience through the needle's eye of the moment.

All adoration, all intercession gathered to a point in the one sustained note.

Standing at the place where the vertical of the Cross bisects time's narrative, Religious become passive conductors for the lightning of God.

The repetition of gesture, phrase, and word—at times a petrified forest, yes, but also the trees with medicinal leaves that bear fruit every month, because they grow on the banks of the river of life.

Psalm 94

The great Invitatory psalm, "Come, ring out your joy to the Lord," sums it all up, stanza by stanza. First, properly, the burst of praise and thanksgiving, followed in the next stanza by the grandeur of God the Creator. Then the small words, "Come in," the longed-for words: in through the gate into the sheepfold, or, as here, to the run on the high hill to which the Lord's sheep are hefted, like the hill sheep of the north country, bred to know where they belong.

There follows the cry, "Oh, that today you would listen to his voice, harden not your hearts!" and the list of infidelities and betrayals that mounts inexorably to the terrible last verse: "Never shall they enter into my rest!" Yet this threat is merely the outer husk of a covert promise. The God of the Old Testament is the God of U-turns, constantly going back on his word, forever repenting. And hidden behind the dark smudge of the bludgeon, but visible to us who stand on the farther side of Golgotha, lies the infant figure of the Redeemer, the One who himself shall be our rest. It was not for nothing that we were bidden to come in and kneel. Praise Him.

God the Creator slays us.
God the Word speaks us.
God the infant hallows our tenderness.
God in dying quickens us.
The risen God names us.
God the Spirit is our guest.

Saint Luke's Little Summer

On the stillest of days, when the October sun was creeping slowly across the untroubled blue of the sky and shadows were walking over the many greens of the garden, I heard a sudden rush among the leaves as an apple detached itself from the branch and fell with a quiet thud. It knew its time.
Even an apple finds the moment bruising.
A late-hatched magpie, small but perfectly feathered, came hopping round my feet. It spied a low-flying insect, made a rush, and caught it, taking it apart with pedantic care before it was ready to be swallowed. Another was found and eaten faster. Before it hopped out of sight the dark blue-mauve of its rump caught the sun's burnish.
A small butterfly, mouse-grey, its forewings spangled with ivory, was perched on the edge of a crater dug by a bird in a large rotten apple. Almost vertical, it was gorging itself on fermented juice, the dark underside of its closed wings lit round the edge by slanted sunlight. Sated, it opened them like a flicked fan, displaying the discreet beauty of the hidden speckles, and flew off into the sun's eye.

Valerian, foxgloves, buddleia, hollyhocks all growing out of walls; grass pushing, down and up, through the hairline cracks in the asphalt of a little-used road: one should never underestimate the power of the Spirit to infiltrate a life where doors and windows appear not only shut but draught-proofed.

iii. Small Talk

Early we receive a call, yet it remains incomprehensible,
and only late do we discover how obedient we were.

Czeslaw Milosz[1]

1. Czeslaw Milosz, "Capri," *New and Collected Poems 1931–2001* (New York: Ecco Press, 2001), 585–88.

Frontier Lands

Whether sleeping or waking he knew not . . .

Other modes of seeing
modes perhaps of being
lie just
outside the field of vision
look away
they are shy
like at dawn a deer
briefly
between wood and field
shade and light
standing clear.

Such will not be caught
in a net of words
or shot
of a sudden
but on the foreshore of sleep
one may come
round a headland
and linger
unbidden.

How this was so, they did
not know (so said they
long ago
and still say so):

just that it was
between two states or modes
but which
they did not know

only that it was so.

Found in Jesus: Lost in God

We are each stretched on the cross of time and space, and our particular point of insertion in the here and now, whether we know it or not, is the heart of Jesus.

Many years ago, when I first discovered the Cistercian Fathers and, through them, monastic theology and a whole new dimension to religious understanding, I met, particularly in Saint Bernard, the notion that devotion to the humanity of Christ was a phase, good but transitory, in an ascent to the spiritual love of the eternal Word. Knowing nothing of either, with facile presumption I decided I was more suited to the latter. Thanks to the God who overlooks our hubris and leads us patiently through the mazes of our own designing, I am happy to go back at the end of my life to the beginning. But to love Christ's humanity one must first learn to love one's own and that of others, which is no less of grace, so that now I ricochet from the human to the divine and back again, never distinguishing clearly which precedes the other, uncaring so long as the goal is sure. Aelred held that it was possible to come to God through pure affectivity: in kissing the feet of Christ we raise our eyes to the Father's face and see the Three in One.

I hear you calling, Lord; like the child Samuel I hear you calling in the night. In the night of the heart, of the soul, of the senses. And I get up to look for you, but because it is night for me, I lose my way. Indeed I do not know it is you.

I follow my pain and my longing and the will o' the wisp of joy down blind alleys, and I fall into a pit and stake myself. And still I hear you calling: you call in the longing that tears me apart; you are the desire and the desired; you are pursuer and pursued. Now that I know it is you, there is no point in my going about the city and seeking you in the streets and in the squares. I have listened to the watchmen. They tell me to go home and sit still: you will look in through the lattice, you will knock at the door, and you will rise like the sun on my darkness. Amen, come, Lord Jesus.

The Riddling Lord

I was pulled back from the brink last night, from the verge of chaos. Into my mind came the words: *He has kept you in the dark*. I understood it at first to mean only that the Lord had kept and was keeping me in a state of unknowing, but then I realized that *kept* had two meanings: he wanted me in the dark and would keep me safe so long as I kept my eyes on him. Below and outside the circle where I stood, and in still deeper darkness, were the lurkers, waiting and wanting me to look at them. If I looked I would give them power; when I ignored them, they shrank and faded. The sense of safety was palpable.

To be in the dark is now my greatest blessing since it is his will. It is to stand in the place of love. And indeed when the words *he has kept you in the dark* came into my mind I had been repeating as an act of will and only half knowing what I was saying: *I will stand in the place of love*. I must not seek meaning. I must not look to either side, nor forward beyond the moment. The meaning is known to him and hidden in his will.

Sometimes I sit on a bare hill in a rain of words, spent words, ink-black, falling through a grey sky. Words arrayed in power, dressed to kill, dressed to please: as in a fairy tale, all have been sent and all have failed the test. Only a few small words, carried by angels and wrapped in silence, will be let through.

◆ ◈ ◆

It can happen that I sit through office filling the entire space, and wrapping the praying community, of which I should be part, in negativity. It is something that comes out of me like an emanation, and in which presumably I connive even as I detest it. It ought to be frightening, but latterly I almost welcome it. It evacuates me from myself. There is no self left for me to indulge, to flatter, to play games with. No possibility of dialogue. No distraction. No room, in a sense, for sin. Just a knowledge that I can get no further from God and that, astonishingly, having come to that frontier, I am where he is—or rather, he is where I am, which is the same thing. It is thus the place of ultimate security.

He doesn't leave me in it through Mass. Perhaps it isn't safe to spend too long there, or perhaps the negative spirit takes fright and flight. But there is something cleansing about being in the cellar. It is the underside of what there are no words for.

Ordinavit In Me Caritatem

I have a lion that is rampant, and unlike Saint Jerome's it will not come to heel. I struggle to get it caged and keep it there, focusing with all my might, like a squinting child in the orthoptist's clinic, but as soon as I take my eye off it or, worse, linger on its beauty, it escapes at a bound into the jungle of my fantasies and fears. There are moments when I quicken at the sound of its roar. But with grace it will be caged, because that is my instant prayer, and one day, when he shall have set all my loves in order in me, it will lie free before the mercy seat, collared only in truth and love.

Let me lay my self to sleep, Lord, in the bottom of your boat, where the rocking will keep it quiet, for it is very childish, and I will sit with you above, where the wind blows. *Ego dormio sed cor meum vigilat.*[2]

Prodigal? Not even. Like the elder son, I've stayed most of my life on the father's farm, but not in the inner garden, slaking my thirst at the fountain by the yew trees—down in an outlying field grumpily hoeing mangolds; but even there the father walked out every day and left me my pittance in the shade of the hedge.

2. Song 5:2.

To walk with God there must be silence within and without. My mind and my heart keep up an incessant chatter. They are like naughty children after bedtime; I cannot keep them quiet, and losing my temper with them has no effect: we all end up worse. Perhaps the only way is to give them a book to read until they go to sleep. Then in the silence I shall hear my God.

When God in his goodness enlarges the heart, he hollows it out to hold love and suffering in equal measure, the two faces of his Son, whose dwelling-place it then becomes. But joy is of the Spirit, a bird of passage, briefly alighting and soon gone.

The acceptance of suffering is prayer. To understand this is a source of rejoicing, for it is the one form of prayer that cannot be denied us by our own weakness or sinfulness. The rejoicing doesn't last, for the suffering must take over again, but the acceptance can.

It is not enough to surrender pain, one must also surrender joy, which can be harder.

Games of Faith

I play this game with you, Lord, in the high top on the trapeze. I am the one who lets go at the sick-making extremity of the swing, and you are the partner hanging with arms extended, waiting to catch me by the wrists. It is odd that I, so fearful of most things, including heights, should find my security with you in outer and inner space.

Lord, I am tired of this losing streak. All you present me with are Snakes, or cards saying Miss 3 Turns, or Go to Jail. If I am to play games with you I want to win. You keep the best cards, the cards of faith, in the pack or up your sleeve for the most part. How can I ever win if you won't deal them out? Do you not *want* mountains moved? There are no faith cards in my hand. My only suit is longing, and there I hold them all, right up to the ace, and when I play I slap them down one after the other, face up on the table; but without a faith card to take the tricks, where does it leave me? When I play for others, those closest to me, those in need, those who ask and those whom, for your own mysterious reasons, you have given me, I play the love cards, the few I have, the small ones of no account—no court cards among them. But when you played with Thérèse and took all her faith cards away, you let love be trumps.

You have battered my heart, three-personed God, you have wheeled up your big siege engine and brought my ramparts tumbling into the ditch. My gates are burst asunder and I have given up the keys. I am an open city, Lord, and your banner over me is love.

When I kneel before the tabernacle, the indwelling Father greets the Son embodied in the host. I am the stillness in which Father and Son converse in the Spirit, and each time a thought swims up into the intervening space it interrupts the love talk of the Trinity.

You have walled me in silence, Lord; I am deep in the well of your high tower. You are my only visitor, for you alone know where I am. Indeed I do not know myself.

The Old Adam and the New

I am two people, always. The infant Christ is for ever being born in me, unheralded, unexpected, undeserved. He slithers naked into my cold air, livid but beautiful. And always there is the old Adam, refusing to give place; a creature of habit, ensconced, as heavy-shouldered as a nightclub bouncer. While I keep my eyes on the infant I am in him, he is in me, and all the world is changed. But as soon as my attention slackens the old inhabiter lumbers in, heavy yet soft-footed, and fills the horizon. He is the invader, to whom I open the gate; the other, begotten in the womb of being. Abide with me, Lord Jesus.

Day by day, year by year I am made aware that there are few things I have despised in others that I have not myself struggled with or stooped to.

I may not, like the Psalmist, wear my pride like a necklace,[3] but I flaunt a selection of vanities like so many strings of imitation pearls.

There are people I wear round my neck like mufflers, and sometimes, feeling suffocated, I am tempted to strip off. Then I have to remind myself smartly that I too am a muffler for

3. *Grail Psalter*, Ps 73:6.

others, and that there are aristocrats out there who wear their mufflers like a fashion garment.

Habitual sinfulness is such a cosy thing, like some old fleece-lined garment, snug-fitting, yet easy at the elbows—it's not surprising that we cling to it. When the unwashed smell drives me now and then to strip it off, I hang it within reach, on the back of the bathroom door; it doesn't stay there long.

There is nothing like the running spectacle of our vanity for keeping us humble.

To be accounted humble would be the highest praise, but if we were we would not hear it.

I am like a lump of dough that a child has played with all day long, grimed through and through. As it is pulled and patted into different shapes new seams and layers of grime are brought to the surface.

The radicality of my weakness and the infinity of his mercy span the whole gamut of the possible.

◆ ◈ ◆

Never more self-referential than when praying.

◆ ◈ ◆

I have a stable full of golden calves and a pedestal for setting them on by turns.

◆ ◈ ◆

All I have ever done is to say yes or no to the invitations of the Spirit, invitations prepared for me before the beginning of the world.

◆ ◈ ◆

I have spent much of my life asserting that I would do God's will if only I knew what it was, and stabbing around with a tail on a pin, trying crossly to get it on the donkey. Had I made a habit of saying "yes" to the small invitations of God ("Shall we go for a walk?" "Would you like to say Lauds?") I wouldn't be lining up convincing excuses when the big ones come along.

◆ ◈ ◆

All things know God's will for them except us. It only became mysterious after Eve took the apple.

◆ ◈ ◆

God's will: the next thing I least want to do.

◆ ◈ ◆

There is always another Yes to be said.

To be an old glove turned inside out and pegged out in rain and wind and sun, so that nothing sticks.

We are told that it is a terrible thing to fall into the hands of the living God. I'd rather fall into the hands of the breaker and maker than into the grip of the minotaur, waiting at the end of every blind alley.

I prayed, "Lord, give me the grace to conduct my life with a bit more dignity." Then, thinking that God wasn't really into dignity, I changed it to humility, on the grounds that the public effect would be much the same and the private vastly better.

To be asked continually for what one doesn't have is worse than having one's own gift returned to sender; it imposes a burden of guilt from which there is no setting free. "I have freed your shoulder from the burden"; yes, yes, from what I owe you, Lord, but how can you set me free from what I owed to others, except in the sense that it was owed to you in them? There is no pain, no loss that cannot be flipped over into joy except the failure to give others their due measure.

Humility and Love

Humility and love are the two essentials, the twin pillars. Neither is a quality, which would predicate them on us, or on God: the first would be ridiculous, the second inconceivable. Nor are they a gift, implying permanency. They are manifestations of grace. Love, in its activity, is a particularity of the Holy Spirit; humility, of Jesus.

We need grace to ask for them, grace to welcome and receive them, and the grace we call wisdom to apply them in context.

If we pray for humility we may expect to be humbled—soon— it will be a sign that our prayer has been heard, for experience is the path we must tread on our way to the uplands.

All so-called virtues are enfolded in them, mere categories and distinctions beloved of the human mind.

They stand at the beginning and end of Saint Benedict's Rule, the two door-openers, the first to life in God, the second to life eternal, which two may be, and in a sense are, concurrent.

◆ ◈ ◆

Love and humility are the only guarantors of remaining in the will of God. If we remain in him, the Spirit will adjust the pattern of our lives at every step we take.

◆ ◈ ◆

Love is a nakedness. I was told once, "Turn your face into the north wind." That is endurance lovingly accepted. But to love without reserve is to let oneself be stripped of everything, including one's vest, and stand naked to whatever blows. That is why Julian of Norwich saw that bitter wind drying the flesh of Jesus on the cross.

Risen with Healing in His Wings

Surely divine forgiveness embraces those we have wounded and extends to them an element of healing, for what is the point of my being forgiven while others suffer the consequences of my sins? The Risen Christ passes with his peace through all our walls, and the pardon won for us on the cross is breathed out as healing in the Spirit, blowing where it wills.

When the Father looks at me he sees only the Son. When the Son looks at me he sees my sinfulness—the pervasiveness and deadly triviality of it—and forgives.

We should carry the weaknesses of others tenderly cradled in our arms, like babies needing to be fed and changed.

Things slip away. Mental energy drains down the plughole, taking with it focus in prayer, the concentration necessary for reciting even one psalm with an adequate degree of meaning. Emotional flatness overlies the land like stagnant floodwater. This does not prevent me carrying a rucksack, like Bunyan's Christian, stuffed with vanity and negative thoughts, and like him I cannot shift the load. Yet there is joy hidden somewhere in such poverty: the pure joy of owing everything, owning nothing, and having—it would seem—no further to fall.

I long for judgment, for the driving storm that sweeps all away, for the cleansing of the earth and myself with it. And after it I hear, "Seek the Lord all you, the humble of the earth, who obey his commands. Seek integrity, seek humility: you may perhaps find shelter on the day of the anger of the Lord."[4] I love with passion the word *perhaps*; it is the word of his mercy. I hold on to perhaps; it is surer than all the superlatives.

My polar opposites are so far apart that I cannot see one from the other. Either I am traveling out, beyond known perimeters, where language fails, towards the non-place of a non-word, which is at once Nothing and All. Or I go inward, along the path of Christ's humanity, to where the body itself is sacramental, to where nothing can be expressed save through that medium, and I, like the woman at his feet, hold all my tenderness in two worn hands.

I am pinned down like a mole skin nailed to a board for curing. Pinned at the four corners and down each edge by inbred genes, by race and by class, by childhood experience, by choices made, by habits good and bad—present and future predicated on the past. And yet in the center of my being lurks this glorious freedom, worshipful, one with the God who made me. Whatever takes place in the final unmaking of body and mind, he will take this freedom into his own keeping, safe from sin, hidden in Christ, wrapped in love.

4. Zeph 2:3.

In failing to address our faults we leave Christ hanging on the Cross, the weight of his body pulling forward on the nails. When we struggle to amend them we are helpers at the deposition, wiping the blood from his feet, holding them close.

Blessed are we, Lord, in your incarnation, for daily we meet your tortured flesh at the place of division. There we come with our wounds and, bleeding, find you there before us. We come there too in our anger and have to push past your hanging body before we can strike our brother. Before Abel was, you are.

Lord, let me live my life in your Beyond, where nothing is coveted nor anything withheld.

Songs of the Spirit

Bede, at the last, rejoiced in the expectation of seeing "Christ in his beauty." Not the man on the cross, without form or comeliness to attract us, nor the risen Christ who could still pass for a gardener or a traveler on the road, but Christ *in his beauty*, Word through whom the universe flowered into being, Wisdom playing with uncreated beauty, face of the Father turned in love towards us. Keats' lines, "Beauty is truth, truth beauty, / This is all we know on earth and all we need to know," which I used to think so inadequate as an epitome of necessary wisdom, open magically like Chinese flowers in cockle shells when placed in this living water.

All our stories are the drone above which the divine melody soars and dances, composing the new song that each of us will sing before the throne. We are the song, we are the instruments the Spirit plays. All will be adoration.

"To the Father, through the Son, in the Spirit," is prayer in a silver nutshell. It is deeply trinitarian. It is also intercessory, for one can place one person after another in that current and send them in trust and with beseeching on their way. It opens a path through silence and yet it is itself silence. Nothing I can conceive of falls outside it.

Adoro te devote, latens Deitas.[5]

Riding pillion behind Saint Thomas in the shelter of his broad back. The Lord's ox needs a Percheron at least to carry him, a very Summa Theologica of a horse, ears pricked, strong in the quarters, hairy-heeled, bred for clopping down the centuries. It will not notice a free-rider on the saddlecloth, and as for Thomas, he is kindly, and anyway he is busy singing.

◆ ◈ ◆

Christ, the swinging door
between heaven and earth
time and eternity
man and God;
knock and it will open.

◆ ◈ ◆

Holy Spirit of God,
open my mind that I may know the Father,
open my heart that I may love the Son,
open my ears that I may hear his voice,
open my eyes that I may see him in the stranger,
open my hands to serve all others in their need,
open my lips to praise the Three in One:
Glory be to the Father, through the Son, and in the Holy
    Spirit,
as it was in the beginning and is and ever shall be,
world without end, amen.

---

5. Thomas Aquinas, Hymn ("Godhead, here in hiding, whom I do adore," trans. Gerald Manley Hopkins).

Advent

Advent watchfulness: a waiting with every sense strained. If we keep our eyes fixed on the dusty road we shall see the Virgin, pregnant with the divine Word, walking towards us. That is the promise. The obverse is no less true: if we doze or flit manically through these weeks, when we look at the crib at Christmas, all we shall see is a celluloid doll.

He was so heavy, Lady, he had grown big in your womb since that March day when the angel came, a sprig of flowering blackthorn in his hand. Now the two of you are rocking and clopping down the rough road to Bethlehem. He is restless now, elbowing you, his world is waiting for the child you carry.

Lady, the world is still rolling on its way, and we, we are still waiting for a coming. There is no one to carry him now, you need some helpers. Stretch out your hand, Lady, year by year, to those called to take your place on the road, in tiredness and discomfort, elbowed by their burden, the love-bearers carrying your Son to the birthing place.

There is a sense in which it is more blessed to be God's mother than to be God. Christ was God by nature, she was the vessel of election by grace, a thing most precious and beautiful to contain him, into which he perfectly fitted.

A woman nursing a baby is the only relationship unaffected by the Fall, all others have to be rebuilt on grace.

The Mind's Eye

I saw in my head a round pool in a formal garden, perhaps ten feet across. Set back from it was a carved stone surround and on it a child sitting, naked and beautiful, her face slightly averted. I was that child, and the water that filled the pool was the loving mercy of God, his *hesed*.

I saw a man sitting, weary and drained. His features in profile were sharp, as though carved by an axe, and his skin was leeched of all color. He was given a glass of water, but I saw no giver, and he raised it and drained it while I watched. And I understood the words *This is the draught of life*. The weariness was his meaning.

Looking out through the window of my mind I saw a landscape, flat, featureless, covered with bodies of the dead and dying, their limbs at grotesque angles. There was no variation of color, just different shades of sepia, the flesh paler. It was a field of conflict. I saw only men, drab in uniform, but they were all humanity. I looked again, and I saw an orchard, a bucolic scene with brilliant greens and red, and blue of sky, like a Book of Hours, but not miniaturized: it had vigor, yet also perfect harmony. I understood that everything I saw looking out was also within, and that these were hell and heaven. And just as there was no difference between out and in, nor was there any between now and forever, because now is for ever and forever will be now.

◆ ◈ ◆

Out of the early morning dark a visualization of the Book of Job swam uninvited into my mind, interrupting a session on the treadmill of family problems. I saw that I/Job was sitting in the middle of the road and God wanted us out of the way. He needed the road clear to let his traffic pass. I meanwhile am sitting there in the road listening to Job's friends in my head saying, "Why me?" and "It's not fair, other people have this . . . other people do that . . . ." Or alternatively, "It's all my fault." Job's wife, Job's friends, parasites always waiting at the door, entering unasked, often let in by me, not only persuasive but addictive.

If I get out of the road, out of the way, the wind of the Spirit will pass, the air will change, the face of the earth will be renewed; as it is at the end of the Book of Job.

I no longer know to whom I owe the word *unwanting*. Wherever it came from, it set off a small turmoil in my mind the other night, which is still unraveling. I caught it as it drifted across the night sky and set it beside unknowing. Both are journeying words, on a road to somewhere. Unknowing, with its attendant cloud, is cool and damp. Unwanting, partnered with desire, took me last night straight to the desert, landscape of purgation, the place where our desires are redirected, given other goals: *ordinavit in me caritatem.*

The only living thing that I saw in this desert was a giant scorpion: it belonged there. Its sole business was inflicting pain—the pain of unfulfilled desire: pain in the craving, and also pain in the renunciation of desire and the learning of unwanting. The sight of the scorpion brought to mind the Stanley Spencer painting, one of four entitled "Christ in the Wilderness." A heavy-bodied Christ is seated on the ground in his robe, knees splayed, feet bare. His coarse hands are laid open, one upon the other, and form a platform for a scorpion. The scorpion in the painting is much smaller than the one in my desert, smaller than I remembered, surprisingly small in actuality. He is looking at it with love. The scorpion has pincers at both ends and its tail is arched over its back, whether in menace or in greeting isn't clear. Christ's eyes stay bent on it, his mouth lost in a thicket of beard. He says: "You don't frighten me, little one, I made you."

Love was first set in order in the desert, that we might be set free. All cravings, whether physical or, more pernicious, for power, attention, misplaced affection—all must be unlearnt through a long apprenticeship to the Master of unwanting. Scorpion of death, scorpion of healing, inflicting the one pain that enslaves or frees, kills or cures, we too must love you, fiery image of the serpent of salvation destined to be nailed for our healing on the Cross.

◆ ◈ ◆

I read the word *nothing* in a reference to *The Cloud of Unknowing,* and at once I saw what seemed to be a doorway standing on a hill against the sky. There was just the empty frame, quite plain, and it was filled with Nothing. I looked on Nothing, which was dove-grey and faintly luminous, and I felt it was adorable, passing any thing. After a brief moment the reality drained out of it, leaving only the memory.

Now the memory too has gone. Perhaps that is why one writes things down.

◆ ◈ ◆

The other night, lying awake, I saw in my mind's eye Christ hanging on the Cross, but all I was aware of was the nailing of the feet and hands; not the pain, but the powerlessness. It was the crucifixion of the will. I had the very strong sense that this was the meaning of it for us, for me—not suffering, but the complete surrender of the will. That of course is a form of suffering.

Days of Preparation

Love's lover gave his breath
for you
for me
a victim racked
his arms outstretched
his hands nailed to the knowledge tree;
from his kind wounds
the bright blood ran down free.

While from another sport
of that same tree
standing across
from Calvary
dangles a dead-weight
swinging, he
the traitor who
is you
is me.

Stretched in a tomb
love's lover lies
near the dutiful roots
of the olive tree;
in linen shroud
his limbs are furled
till love shall quicken in stone womb
the mortal flesh, immortal food
for me
for you
for all his world.

iv. The Sheep of His Flock

And I saw the river over which every soul must pass to reach the kingdom of Heaven. And the name of that river was Suffering. And I saw the boat which carries souls across the river. And the name of that boat was Love.[1]

---

1. Of uncertain authorship, widely but mistakenly attributed to Saint John of the Cross.

Intercession

The small hours are the busy hours
on the night's freeways.
Before the first cock crows, before
the advent thrush punctures the heavy dark,
before the headache opens an eye
the sleepers rise and walk,
those stretched out underground and those
laid warm between the sheets.

For these hours are the watching hours
in restless beds
when such as wake keep vigil
for the living and the dead
and call by name
friends lovers mothers sons
to heave them in their outstretched minds
over eternity's dark rim.

And these hours are night's noon-
day of delight
when all the nameless hearing themselves called
come hurrying from west and east
to houses churches chapels cells where they
are dressed in prayer
and given oil-lamps filled and trimmed
to light them to a feast.

Inner Weather

Our only gift to God is attention. It is a very clean state of being, independent of love-as-feeling, which is as fickle as the English weather and even less predictable.

Whereas our so-called good works are bedeviled by mixed motives, at best opportunities responded to, attention is a movement of the will, ideally involving body, mind, and heart; it thus brings the whole being into unity.

Fervor is God's gift to us, not ours to him.

A state of drought is preferable to a spate of emotion: it rules out self-flattery.

He will send rain in due season. There is a drought that is of God and a drought that is of us; the latter comes of a failure to dig the irrigation channels and put out basins to catch the rain when it comes. God never sends a drought unless he knows we have enough reserves and that the seed is safe.

When God puts us to the test he sends grace in sufficient measure, since he wants us to succeed. It is when we put ourselves to the test that we fail most dismally.

◆ ◈ ◆

We are conduits for grace, and most of all in our flaws and weaknesses. As grace flooded the world through the wounds of Christ, so it trickles through ours.

◆ ◈ ◆

If we trust enough we shall be led blindfold through the labyrinth of temperament, sprung like Saint Peter from prisons of our own and others' making, and even when fettered we shall know ourselves free.

I Put Myself in Your Hands

The act of homage: the submission in trust of one man to another: hands placed in hands. The self-giving of Christ in the host: so powerfully symbolic. What better reason for keeping the option of reception in the hand? Only infants have food placed directly in their mouths by an intermediary, and refusal is one of their first steps towards autonomy. Christ was not coy with his Body and Blood at the Last Supper. He handed it over. Literally. Even to Judas. Specially to Judas.

Prayer: time spent in the Presence, allowing the Holy Spirit to unravel the narrative we have knitted up since our last visit. Passive? No, for the Spirit always needs our co-operation. And the more time we spend there the less knitting we shall do in between.

We may have no idea of where we are going in life, yet we can have some confidence that we are headed in the right direction, since, in Saint Augustine's words, "before telling [us] whither, he told [us] by what way." "I am the way, he said," to which Augustine added his favorite recommendation, that we must carry on walking,[2] it was the walking that mattered. Better still for Augustine was to walk and sing. He

2. Saint Augustine of Hippo, *Homilies on St John's Gospel*, Treatise 14, 8–9.

would have been happy if he'd been out and about in rural Oxfordshire in 1915:

> By the time I were thirteen I were already working the land set to the plough, sometimes on my own with not a soul in sight, sometimes with other teams in concert. A strong bond was felt between boy, man and carter, and with those who had trod the earth before us, and on a crisp morning when the tilth were turning easy, and we could lift our eyes at times from the dark earth to the sunlit uplands, a leading voice 'ud launch on the still frosty air:
>
> *When the trumpet of the Lord shall sound and time shall be no more*
> *And the morning breaks eternal, bright and fair,*
> *When the saved of the earth shall gather over on the farther shore,*
> *And the roll is called up yonder we'll be there . . .*
>
> And we *were* there, soprano, tenor, bass, taught to harmonize in church, chapel, and pub, turning our steaming teams in jingling unison. Snatching a breath to give our last echo a chance to catch up over the new-ploughed furrow, we'd roll forth again across the listening landscape:
>
> *When the roll (when the roll) is called up yonder*
> *When the roll (when the roll) is called up yonder*
> *When the roll is called up yonder——WE'LL BE THERE!*[3]

And if the poor of the earth shall inherit the kingdom, then who would doubt it?

---

3. *Lifting the Latch, a Life on the Land,* as told to Sheila Stewart, by Mont Abbott of Church Enstone, Oxfordshire (Charlebury, Oxon, UK: Day Books, 2003), 49.

Forgiveness

God does not require our repentance. It is we who need it, in order to open ourselves to the cleansing power of judgment and the healing of forgiveness.

Forgiveness in our culture (including that of the Church) is seen as a reward for due apology, even as pardon and absolution are contingent on repentance and confession. Yet apology is a prime example of mixed motives, too often offered with a self-interested end in view (who does not remember childhood apologies ground out through gritted teeth and avoiding eye contact, which spoke more of defiance than regret?).

The parable of the prodigal son teaches a quite different lesson, namely that apologies play a peripheral part in the story of forgiveness. The apology of the straying son was entirely self-serving. It was thought up in that "far country" we all know, as a way out of broken dreams and present discomfort, and trotted out on arrival the minute he drew breath after his father's unexpected embrace. But his father didn't bother to reply, he had already passed on to the welcome and the feast.

This father, from the moment he glimpsed his son a long way off down the dusty road, "was filled with pity." He didn't think, "This will teach him a lesson; it's time he learned that bad behavior has consequences; a bit of groveling will do him good." It was pity alone that dictated his reaction: pity for the young man's present state of moral and material wretchedness. And the cure? A bear-hug, a kiss, a bath, clean clothes, a splendid meal.

It isn't an easy place to start from when one isn't God, particularly as we share in the moral wretchedness of those we view as owing us apologies, but it is surely the place we are called to.

This is not to deny the proper place of contrition when we have offended either God or neighbor, but there are other parables, starting with the publican and the Pharisee, to teach us that. It may well be that the prodigal son plumbed the depths of contrition *after* his father's loving embrace, rather than before. All divine truths are multi-faceted, and every angle of approach needs to be explored, above all the seemingly contradictory.

If we die leaving our brother, daughter, friend with the wrong they have done us unforgiven, not only are they left with this burden to carry forward for as long as they live, we also leave them the knife-edge of our rancor to twist in the wound. It is a form of control exerted beyond the grave, not unlike suicide in certain conditions. The will is a limpet.

We all want to have the last word. If we knew it, we might be less keen. It is forgiveness.

Self and Others

Human beings in a state of nature tend to be bullies or manipulators, and most of us are both in differing degrees: bullies
with those weaker than ourselves, manipulators when faced
with those who have power over us. To conduct one's relation-
ships in the rigor of total truth is the hardest thing to do. We
have first to acknowledge using—and then renounce—a lifetime's tactics of self-preservation; next to lay aside the secret
weapons we rely on to get our way with those who enjoy a
psychological advantage (or on whom we have conferred it),
and finally walk naked to meet them without arms or armor.
It is not so much that it is frightening; it is the impossibility
of ridding oneself of habits so ingrained that they lie below
the surface of the skin. Only grace is systemic.

To be thanked for a service we have rendered enables us to
grab a counterweight of satisfaction, and in doing so we have
had our reward. We should rather be thankful for the oppor-
tunity given us. The Gospel's extra mile lies inward.

A sudden flash of understanding needs to be embodied over
time through repetition.

To consider the motives of others, where necessary, in the light of Christ's love; to explore one's own motives, constantly, in the light of Christ's truth.

◆ ◈ ◆

The sense of injury and the perception of slights come trickling out of the leaking cistern of vanity that admiration keeps topped up. The whole thing is a mirage.

◆ ◈ ◆

Nine times out of ten it is better to say nothing. The tenth is the time we choose to keep silence.

◆ ◈ ◆

One should never speak out of hurt, for the only voice that comes out of hurt is anger.

◆ ◈ ◆

There is a path that leads from self-sufficiency through the desolation of loneliness—into which pit one can stumble very suddenly—to the peace of being alone with God. And since all things find their source and home in him, to be alone with him is to be intensely present to others.

◆ ◈ ◆

Sadly, in conversation we rarely say anything that is worth saying. And yet those things are there, trembling on the edge of silence, waiting to be born.

◆ ◈ ◆

It is years since I struggled with Eckhart and eventually put him to one side. His teaching that the uncreated God was the only proper object of our love, that all creatures should be loved only in him, was too hard, too inhuman, or so I told myself, going to hide him on a top shelf already stocked with other set-asides. But I knew it was a failure: mine, not his. I just preferred not to think about him.

I now know that all love that is not totally self-giving is in some part, great or small, about our own needs, however we dress them up (and some of us are very skilled at the art). We all have hopes that turn into expectations and finally, if we are not careful, into entitlement. The only remedies are vigilance and grace: vigilance that looks to prayer, prayer that opens the way for grace. Grace allows us to step first into a place of freedom: if *I* am not free, how can I loosen the bonds of those I am trying to tether to myself? Freed from wanting, I cease to make demands and love can flourish.

This freedom is not indifference, real, feigned, or self-deceiving. Indifference is another cul-de-sac, another flight from hurt, another armoring—worse perhaps than anger because more deceitful.

Indifference is undone by intercession. Intercession unlocks hearts—the hearts of those who think themselves, may indeed wish themselves, indifferent. Whether it unlocks the hearts of those we pray for is perhaps a proper matter for indifference. Prayer is never a matter for self-congratulation: its outcomes are all hidden in God, they are holy ground.

Love is always moving on, passing from heart to heart, never captive, rarely returned as one would wish. To seek to stop it on its way, to appropriate it to oneself, is to pervert its nature. What comes to one, undeserved, must be passed swiftly on, and what one gives from the heart should be given lightly and no dues exacted. The only love one may properly keep for oneself is that of God, and in that one may rest.

◆ ◈ ◆

If we fulfilled our duties there would be no need of rights. The emphasis on rights empties relationship of its only true basis, which is love. It introduces an element of competition and reclamation where there should be only giving, but in a sinful world rights, and the law to back them up, are a necessary protection.

Rights are for others, entitlement is for Me.

Similarly, were we all obedient to God, and to Christ in each other, there would be no need of authority, still less of control. Control is the consequence and also the source of sin. Ideally it protects. Too often it corrupts the controller and abuses the controlled. And there will never be any escape from this openness to sin; our only defense is everlasting vigilance.

"The health and character of community is dependent on the quality of solitudes that make it up."[4]

We are not what we think we are.
We are not what others think we are.
We are not the sum of what we have done.
We are not the sum of what has been done to us.
Alternatively we are all these, and the sum does not add up.

4. Maggie Ross, *Silence: A User's Guide* (Portland, OR: Cascade Books, 2014), I, p. 26.

Self and the Spirit

Self-analysis is not always a sharp enough tool for digging out the truth about ourselves, such is our capacity for self-delusion. Only the presence and power of the Holy Spirit can reveal the Truth in us that is the in-dwelling Christ.

Virtue in ourselves, were we to have it, would be invisible. If we fancy we see it we may be sure that we are looking at a mirage conjured up by vanity (a fault with a great gift for passing unnoticed). Our virtues as perceived by vanity combine to form the flattering self-image we exhibit to friends, and even to strangers, secretly watching for them to reflect it back. True virtue, the presence of the Holy Spirit in the soul, is always unseen and mostly unfelt.

Meeting one's self-image face to face and recognizing it as one's own creation is a gift of the Spirit and, like all his gifts, has a searing power. Once the cherished self-image has been burnt out by the Spirit's flame, it leaves a void, the void our Advent God longs to fill. In this emptiness there is nothing to be sought, not even himself. The Bride in the Song of Songs wasted her time running round the city searching for him. "Go back home," said the watchmen. She went and she sat, with her attention trained on her desire, until she realized he was there, in the empty room, waiting.

Innocence and Innocents

"Because I am little and you love me"—small child to father, to justify being given what she has just asked for: a Thérèsian theology of the Little Way? Not quite, perhaps—what we think of as childhood innocence is already manipulative: it has to be in order to survive and quickly learns sophistication (Thérèse, looking back, came to recognize it in her outgrown self). Once the child can say this, make this claim, she knows that she is on the way to being all-powerful. Behind it one hears the echo of the Gospel words, "Unless you become like little children . . . ." Children cease very young to be little, perhaps they never are and being little is a matter of becoming, of dropping the "because." We *are* little, we *are* loved; these are truths, there is no predication. God does not do things "because"; *il est la gratuité même*, both giver and gift. We are invited to become like him, open-hearted, open-handed. He is uncalculating because all-knowing; we are called to be uncalculating because we know nothing. Innocence does not precede sin, it will come as the last gift, when even the memory of sin has been washed away.

Holy Innocents. No feast is so dependent on its place in the calendar as this. Without the birth of the child in Bethlehem, naked, homeless, threatened, this "feast," this contradiction in terms, would spell the death of God: no God can stand before the massacre of the innocent. But in the vulnerabilities on view in the stable the Cross is already present, opening the door to belief, acceptance, adoration.

◆ ◈ ◆

"That strain again": we have Saint Agnes' Day, and the reading from Saint Ambrose, for which this generation has first to cleanse the mind, while struggling to return to some prelapsarian state where the bodies of children evoke only wonderment and a tenderness coupled with respect. Three concelebrants at mass, the stoles of two running in bright red rivers down the white of their albs, the third standing between them, arms outstretched, as it were soaked in the blood of the child whose feast it is. Less than four weeks ago the Church was asking us to rejoice in the martyrdom of the Innocents—the same Church that has been guilty or connived in the abuse of so many. What a sum of sin is at the source of this continual outpouring. I am knotted with the contradiction between the horror and the celebration.

A blackbird singing is always new, however often we hear it. It is new not only in its spontaneity but because it is singing exactly what God intended it to sing, without either art or artifice. Yet at that rate we should grant the same privilege to the magpie, however much we may detest its triumphant rattle, too often announcing that it has found another bird's nestlings. This is hard, and far, far harder for anyone who has watched as a child the unforgettable emergence of ichneumon parasites from within the body of a pet caterpillar, leaving it voided as they squirm away. Did God really intend this? Darwin could not persuade himself that a beneficent and omnipotent God would have designedly created insects with such habits. That Darwin had a point, God will surely have recognized. The only answer I have been given is: Look at the Cross. I still ask, Why?

Rockabye Baby

Strange that we rock our newborn to sleep by soothing them
with peril,
   When the wind blows the cradle will rock,
swiftly followed by calamity:
   When the bough breaks the cradle will fall,
   Down will come cradle, baby and all.

This feels as old as time and as wide as the world. The French
two-year-old perched on its mother's knee is introduced to
death by drowning—or perhaps just a wetting—by the ferry-
man who offers passage across the river in his petit bateau.
"Paierez-vous? non? Eh bien, coulez, coulez, coulez, coulez!"
These rhyme games are possible because the singer is the parent, usually the mother, whose encircling arms are the very
source of safety. Since trust in the parent is greater than dread
of the danger, which the parent also briefly acts out, the fear
is manageable, squeals of delight are in order.

   The vocabulary of wind and water, storm and flood is also
that of the Psalms, in which God stoops down and seizes us
out of the waters of chaos; like a tender parent he saves us
because he loves us. But in life we mostly float, marooned
for longish periods on the ocean of doubt without a sail or a
palm tree in sight, rocked, when lucky, in the arms of faith.
The precarious balance of rockabye baby is learned in earliest
childhood, but at some moment we have to crash to earth with
the bough, get thrown into the river, follow Christ through
the underworld, if we hope to find ourselves in the beyond
of safety—the safety of beyond.

Is-ness

Animals have an is-ness that humans lack. They are complete in themselves, without exception beautiful with the beauty that comes of being perfectly adapted to their ends. All animals in their natural state fulfill the purpose for which they were destined in the creative mind. The fact that they arrived at this state through a process of evolution is not so much irrelevant as indifferent. In domestic animals this is-ness is diminished by their closeness to humans, their subjection to human needs and their breeding for specific purposes. Animals can be corrupted by both breeding and handling, and the closer they are to us the more vulnerable to corruption they become.

Those animals that lose in some degree their is-ness through contact with human beings participate correspondingly in this openness to another state of being. Those that share our lives most closely and are loved in truth and with integrity of heart learn new responses, embarking in their turn on an apprenticeship of love. It is always a slippery and dangerous path, and animals, unlike us, have no choice of whom they serve. They have therefore a special innocence: not innocence lost, but innocence stolen from them, which makes cruelty to animals particularly loathsome.

Body Language

Sheep with their small hooves measured out for me the length
of the word shepherd. It was longer than I had thought.
The glairy lamb, lying still and unlicked in its slack pelt,
gave it its dead weight. The homing of ewes at dusk
to racked hay nosed and snatched at, troughs lipped clean,
the cud's contemplative meander through paunch

and gut, spelled the word out in many scripts
but only the one language.

We have no is-ness; we are a perpetual becoming. Whereas
a tiger is born, we are made, and in most of us the making
process is still incomplete when death takes us, however late.
Genes determine our specificity, but we are born as something
larval, our potential still uniquely undetermined as to its final
form, grace the channel through which its meaning is infused.
When the Greek Fathers wrote about "divinization," was it not
this that they had in mind? Evolution is in our case not just a
biological process: we are poised between states of being and
given the choice of where we wish to belong.

"I have to find out who I really am." This has become a universal aspiration, heard even on the lips of people who have
passed half a lifetime in the religious life. The heresy of the
self-styled Me generation? We cannot find out who we are,
because as yet we are not. We shall all be harvested, but not
all will be ripened in this life. Some, perhaps much, of the
ripening may take place in the eternal moment when we look
into the face of Christ.

God alone knows who we are; it is his will that we should
become this or that beloved person, and he alone can enable it.

Our bodilyness is all-embracing, totally pervasive. All the centuries that saw the body as imprisoning a quasi-separate soul
saw it also as the great deceiver, the purveyor not of truth,
but of illusion. To combat and correct the misinformation of
the senses, the soul/spirit had reason and revelation to call

upon. Now that our understanding of our make-up is more nuanced and complex, that reason is suspect, and that even our openness to faith is seen as possibly written in our genes, we should learn to cherish our embodiedness instead of either despising or idolizing it. It is tenderness that we need to learn, the tenderness of God towards all created things, the tenderness that finds expression in our hands: hands that make and build, and fondle and soothe—and slap and strangle and kill.

◆ ◈ ◆

"Don't cling to me, Mary," you said. Well, what did you expect? She was the clinging sort. We all are in one way or another. "Just like the ivy," trilled the Victorian bride, "I'll cling to you." Promise or threat? From birth to the grave we cling—to mothers, lovers, children, friends; artifacts; past, present, and even future. I've seen the old cling, not to breath, but to a spectral afterlife on earth by controlling the memories others have of them—the last little game we play.

But now that you are beyond our bodily reach, now, surely, we may cling. Gilbert of Hoyland says so: "If you have sought and found and thrown your arms round your beloved, then hold him fast: hold him, cleave to him . . . for he who cleaves to God will become one spirit with him."[5]

---

5. Gilbert of Hoyland, "Sermon 11 on the Song of Songs," trans. Pauline Matarasso, *The Cistercian World* (London: Penguin Classics, 1993), 219.

That They May Be One

If we are one, then life is a continuum through time as well as space, and it is our human vocation to extend that unity, bringing into shared life every member of our common body. Prayer for the dead, known and unknown, descends into Sheol with the living Christ and is empowered by him. But there are paths into the past with wicket gates, which sidestep death, and it is the job of historians and archaeologists to go in and out and act as resurrectionists on our behalf, delving in documents and artifacts and earth to free those entombed there, restoring them to us to be embraced in understanding. It goes without saying that it should be done with respect: scholarship, like everything else, is easily abused. Even our lumber rooms of individual memory should be kept swept and dusted, for in space and time, through other lives, we extend our own, growing ever in love, as we wait for the time beyond time when all will be gathered together in the One.

I have an ambivalent attitude to "sharing." Of course those who have wisdom or insights should share them. Anything that is in short supply—laughter in particular—should be shared. But too often what we share with great generosity is our toothache, our flu symptoms, our upsets. A joy shared, laughter shared, bring an increase; there is something miraculous about it, a distribution of loaves and fishes. With suffering, physical or emotional, what we are really doing is asking for sympathy, an input of love as a counterweight to pain. This, quite rightly, underlies the nursing of the sick and listening in love to others' grief, the calming of anxieties, the smoothing and soothing of chafed feelings. We need, though, to be wary of abusing the process and displaying our wounds like beggars at the roadside. If we had the courage to open ourselves to the other not as we would like to be seen but as we are, we would lay bare also the negative side, not what has been done to us, but what we have done: in other words, not, See, I have suffered, but, Look, I have hurt.

Father Matthew, at 85, is a man of large benevolence. It shows in the unwrinkled smoothness of the skin on his broad face. It looks out through his wide-set hazel eyes. He tells me with tranquil detachment about his career as an alcoholic, which began when a nun offered him a rum and tequila in the Caribbean and flourished for some thirty years until he was picked out of an English gutter with several broken bones; he still doesn't know how he got there. Father Matthew is well traveled, as befits a friar, and his benevolence, which starts at home (his father was a lovely man, though being Irish he had a little trouble with the drink), encompasses many nationalities. Lovely people, the Norwegians. And the Swedes. And the Finns. Very Lutheran, of course, but then Luther had a lovely side to him. And they all have a terrible problem with alcohol (except perhaps Luther, he is not specific here), as do the Poles. But not Father Matthew any longer. His benevolence embraces them all. A lovely man.

End Time

> Does the road wind up-hill all the way?
> Yes, to the very end.[6]

Indeed, uphill all the way on a downward slope.

♦ ◈ ♦

> But beauty vanishes, beauty passes
> However rare, rare it be.[7]

Though not, they say, the beatific vision. Yet for us time-chained creatures, subject in our bodies to laws of growth and decay, observing mutability in all that surrounds us, the concept of eternity is so alien as to be almost uncongenial. See Naples and die, said someone. See Jerusalem and die? This idea of seeing and dying is a way round fears of satiety and loss, both products of time. The most beautiful things in life are among the most fleeting. It hurts to look at cherry blossom knowing that it will be snatched away. Since nothing will wait on our looking we prefer not to look at all, or to pull our eyes away and cheat time, the cheater. There is also the more terrible fear of our own weariness, of the unsustainability of joy, of finding that our proper place is in the humdrum. Loss has a certain grandeur, satiety has none: Christians have always known that, even if the Romans forgot it.

♦ ◈ ♦

6. Christina Rossetti, "Up-hill."
7. Walter de la Mare, "An Epitaph."

What the old see as problems with time and memory: the difficulty of finding one's place in linear time, and the intermingling of past and present, particularly who is dead and who is not (strange, too, how some we have known can seem more dead than others, how some we embalm, while the most loved live on), may indicate a growing awareness of eschatological time, a blurring of the boundaries and a readying of the soul for the passage into the *eschaton*. This is not to deny physical changes in the brain, but the relation between body, mind, and spirit being mysterious, there seems to be no good reason why parallel interpretations of the process should not be equally valid, each throwing light on the other.

As dealing with the various aspects of linear time necessary for daily living becomes ever more stressful, thinking eschatologically, after the manner of Ephrem the Syrian, can be restorative, bringing tranquility and making for space in the head.

As all the horizons draw in, those of possibility and even of desire, as the springs of energy fail, leaving body and mind inadequate to their usual purposes, all that is left is the spring in the heart of the garden, the fountain welling up to eternal life. Here is the true water of desire, which makes us long for the one Good, for reconciliation, for love without boundary or blemish, for the Companion of the present and eternal Now. May our prayer be, not that this spring may never fail—it cannot—but that awareness of it may remain, that the heart's attention may be fixed on the play of its water and our spirit continue drinking at that source.

Whatever is received from God as gift can be handed back or passed to another, in love, as love: even death.

◆ ◈ ◆

As we walk through the portal of old age we are handed the clothing of indignity and pain. It comes cut out, the pieces roughly pinned, and it's up to us to sew them together with whatever skills we have, and—more importantly—have practised. Arthritic fingers and failing sight are no help. Mercy will be needed.

◆ ◈ ◆

Winding Sheet

There is no vaccine against pain,
no prophylactic for indignity,
no right to choose
another way, no place to hide;
only the handed cup to drain, brimful and spilling
down the ruched front of the unlaundered blouse.

The past is present as
and when it chooses.
Old-fashioned children peep
round doors and beckon,
their hands like pecking birds.
The present's past; its many children merge
into one moon-like face, their who and how sunk deep.

Yet deeper still and stiller lies the self,
shawled like a nursling laid to sleep,
wound round in love as in a sheet (the last)
to save the limbs from twitching
when the hyena stalks that gnaws the heart.

Death is the one test that we are guaranteed to pass. There is of course a wide range of marks for style, etc., awarded by those who have not yet sat the examination, but no candidate has been known to fail. Last night I found this quite comforting. High marks, though, go to Christian Bobin, for another conjuring trick with received wisdom: "Don't you think it is rather splendid, this life where we can do nothing but fail?"[8]

Herbert McCabe, O.P., apparently wrote that the life of the Trinity was an eternal waste of time. Christian Bobin would agree, although he tends to see God in his singularity rather than his tripartness.

It makes a change from the idea of God laboring so hard that he needs to take a day of rest, giving us a pattern consecrated by time. Time is of course the critical factor here. If God is beyond time and space, what can he "do" in any meaningful sense? Action is surely expressed in time, be it nano-seconds or light years, and God is outside time, rendering all attempts to define his action or non-action at best metaphorical. But the pattern was set early on in the stone of the fourth commandment,[9] with the emphasis on labor and—particularly in Protestant England—a fear of the day of rest, which had to be made laborious in its own way by sermon-reading. But the fear of idleness didn't wait on the Puritans. The Desert knew it, and thanks to Saint Jerome it enjoyed phenomenal

---

8. Christian Bobin, "C'est assez beau, cette vie où on ne peut rien faire qu'échouer, tu ne crois pas?" In *Noireclaire* (Paris: Gallimard, 2015), 13.
9. Exod 20:9.

"shares" down the centuries as a proverb: "The devil finds work for idle hands."[10]

Our kind, of course, never does nothing: we breathe to survive, even in sleep. We also, unlike God, have the privilege of wasting time, since God has made us the gift of an unspecified amount. Wasting time and doing nothing are often conflated. In fact we very rarely use time to do nothing; Bobin is right, that is too difficult. What we really mean by the expression is nothing deemed *useful*, or *productive*. And indeed, as we get older and energy drains away, we tend to waste our shrinking ration of time more and more. All the things we meant to do, given time, all the books we swore we'd read, have become too demanding; knitting and sewing are too fiddly for old fingers, and we take refuge in passive occupations, the junk food of the mind. The saints among us pray. Prayer, like doing nothing, is very difficult; it also takes energy, and that well is dry. I can see no way through this desert except quiet pleading. Quiet, because fuss is counter-productive, while pleading pleases a God whose delight is in giving. "Holy Spirit, hear my prayer," repeated as a mantra, will take us a day's journey. It is the equivalent of writing a check to a charity and leaving them to send it where the need is greatest. While we have breath we still have money in the bank: patience is golden guineas, not small change. The Spirit, meanwhile, is the receiving charity, Love Everlasting, from whom all good things come.

The small hours are the great ones: to lie awake through them is to be blessed. The days are a never-ending wrestling with

10. Saint Jerome, "Always have some work on hand, that the devil may find you busy" ("Letter to Rusticus," in *Letters of St. Jerome* 125:11; www .newadvent.org/fathers/3001125.htm).

ourselves, in which we take fall after fall after fall, but there are nights in which every loss is made good. Sleeping pills are a way of shutting the door on God. The old, above all, do not need them. With luck they can make up the loss after lunch.

Prayers, as opposed to prayer, may take on a new life. When failing energy leaves us wordless, the old familiars seemingly blunted by repetition, the psalms, however few, known by heart, the childhood hymns looked down on and forgotten, all return and open to our gaze like sea anemones in untroubled pools.

I have loved more than I knew
And suffered more than I could
I've given more than I had
All is done, all is said.
    Time to go.[11]

---

11. Marie Noël, *Auxerre et Marie Noël*, Société des Sciences Historiques et Naturelles de l'Yonne (Paris: Zodiaque, 1992), 36, translated by Pauline Matarasso.

Lacrimae Rerum

Who knows the longing of the old, except themselves? Who could imagine it? What have the old to long for? I myself who long so often to the point of tears could never have conceived it. The young think that they long, but mostly they don't. How can one long without experience, long when one hasn't known the lack? It was not with longing, but with an agony of impatience, that as a child I waited in the theater for the curtain to go up: up on the unknown, the real world, the infinite possibilities and promises of life. Israel grew old waiting for the Messiah; it was in the desert that Moses learned the meaning of longing, and died of it looking on the Promised Land. Simeon was as old as his people's longing: in all the years of all their generations he held out his arms to the Christ-child, until, cradling him, he could die.

We, who look back to the promise, want more: we long for its fulfillment, for what Moses glimpsed on Sinaï to be made manifest in glory, and for that we too must die. In the meantime the old long for what we know we cannot have here or now: for love without measure given and received; for the end of suffering—less ours than the world's. Each winter we long for spring more intensely, which each year shows to be more fleeting. In us the whole world weeps, secretly, secretly.

◆ ◈ ◆

These last times are offered us as a time of healing, of ourselves and others. I have seen the ailing and failing become the healers. At this time most especially it is laid in their hands to be the healers of the past, and thus also of the future. Tenderness begets tenderness.

Held safe in the darkness of Unknowing like an unborn child in the womb, eyes tight shut.

When we get pushed, reluctant, through the birth canal of death, we shall be truly delivered.

♦ ◈ ♦

Our lives are like the knitting little girls embark on for the new baby: full of loose ends and holes and dropped stitches and chocolate biscuit smears, and it ends up on the teddy. But when the needles have fallen from our hands, someone in that passage will pick up our dropped stitches and wash out the stains, and we shall find that we have knitted wedding garments.

v. Afterword

A collection of random jottings laid open to view requires
some validation or at least excuse. I can only offer it the form
of a story, which I shall tell as baldly as I am able.

It began in 1998, and I wrote the following paragraph the
same day:

> I was kneeling in front of the tabernacle this morning,
> having attempted to empty my mind. The result is rarely a
> state of prayer, more a freewheeling nothingness in which I
> doze off, even at seven in the morning. On the fuzzy screen
> in my head there appeared the words Teach your faith.
> *Teach* had a capital T. On coming back to myself, I asked,
> "Lord, what faith?" I was disturbed and fearful, aware
> that I had nothing to impart. In doubt as to what it meant
> and whether indeed it meant anything at all, I went off
> to Mass and heard in the reading, "I have taught you laws
> and customs, for you to observe in the country of which
> you are going to take possession. . . . But take care, as
> you value your lives! Do not forget the things which you
> yourselves have seen, or let them slip from your heart as
> long as you live; teach them rather to your children and
> your children's children."[1]

1. Deut 4:5-9.

Although writing was a part of my life, the subjects had always been impersonal, and the idea of keeping any sort of journal would have been wholly unattractive. What about, anyway? But it happened that over the next ten or fifteen years I found myself in danger of being overwhelmed by life and burrowed deeper and deeper into God in an attempt to keep my balance. These jottings are the outcome. They were usually written under inner pressure in a process of faith striving for understanding. I have always felt they were not mine, but given, and that therefore they should not be retouched or tampered with. From time to time I have gone through with a weeding fork; anything that didn't meet certain criteria went in the wheelbarrow: the banal, the self-indulgent, whatever struck me as having no validity beyond the personal. There comes a point where one realizes, with texts as with gardens, that if one carries on weeding there will be nothing left. I was looking at that possibility when I was given another nudge. I read a year ago at Easter the following blog post on the appearance of the risen Jesus to Mary Magdalene:

> What happens next is a lesson for us all. Mary is told not to cling to Jesus but to go and tell the disciples what she has seen . . . . Whatever graces we may be given, whatever insight or understanding we may be granted, is not for ourselves alone, but we lay our insights and understanding before the Church, that they may be verified. We, too, are just messengers.[2]

As it was written by someone I greatly respect, I gave it weight and proceeded to separate the texts out according to post hoc themes. Surprisingly they fell, almost of themselves, into four sections of similar length. In this arrangement, what was written for no one I now offer, with great hesitation, to anyone.

---

2. D. Catherine Wybourne, *ibenedictines.org*, Easter Tuesday, 2015.

Reading Between
the Lines

Reading Between the Lines

We have more languages at our disposal than we are always aware of, certainly more than we use consciously and often. Those spoken by our neighbors, near and far, which, if we knew them, would broaden our minds and expand our hearts. Technical languages like mathematics that we leave to experts and the machines at supermarket check-outs, forgetting that fluency in mathematics and cutting-edge physics opens a door to outer space. Closer to home and friendlier is the language of the natural world, the extraordinary ordinary. It is learned by looking with close attention, often. It is the *lectio divina* of divine glory, and the book is free. There is also a language we have half forgotten, the language of the oral tradition that passed unwritten down uncounted generations, the treasure chest of human knowledge packed with the stories that explained us to ourselves. Printing, followed by the growth of literacy, saw by the middle of the nineteenth century the final phasing out of this oral tradition in England. Nonetheless, much of the material, the stories and the language they are told in, remains to us either as literature—texts more often studied than read—or as tales for children, read aloud as such tales should be, and thus still shared and heard.

The Scriptures too, both Hebrew and Christian, were part of that oral tradition and in more than one sense still are, being proclaimed and listened to collectively. All share themes drawn from a common pool of giants and dragons, boy heroes, magic cauldrons, and a conviction that, at a moment of crisis, any rule, including what we would now call the laws of nature, is subvertible (by whom or what, in fairy tales, is not always obvious). More important, they share a belief in good and evil and their mutual opposition, in rewards and punishment, and in the ultimate triumph of the good. Myths and legends introduce the tragic, fairy tales the ghoulish; humanity likes a bit of tragedy, particularly when there is another page to turn: Roland dies at Roncevaux, but Charlemagne will come to avenge him. Children are both less and more sensitive: they enjoy being threatened with indescribable horrors their parents would never cope with (being cooked and eaten by witches), but they also need to be saved in the nick of time, preferably by their own guile. My seven-year-old son, being read a version of *La Chanson de Roland,* dissolved into tears: "J'aime pas les histoires où tous les Français mourent," he sobbed a trifle ungrammatically. He would never have cried over Hansel and Gretel, though he might have been seriously frightened.

We don't believe in legends now; we certainly don't believe in fairy tales, and to save our children from nightmares we assure them that they aren't true—but children know better. We, their parents, have science to guide us, and it has closed our minds to the possibility of other possibilities. Scripture of course is all about possibilities other than the scientific and rational, and the ways in which we approach these and solve the difficulties that they now present are various. Christians position themselves on a spectrum of belief that stretches from a deadening literalism to a point where any historical content that lacks an archeological substratum is vaporized as metaphor. Medieval historians faced with saints' lives are often experts at dissection: having stripped out the useful parts that help them prove how our forebears *really lived,* they toss the rest in the bin labelled "superstition."

We still read fairy tales, usually for their Freudian insights. Some read myths and legends, and of all these genres we are more accepting than we are of religious texts. When we apply the words *myths* or *fairy tales* to the latter it is to dismiss them as rubbish, or worse. Might it be that we just need to re-learn how best to read them all from looking at the elements they have in common? Some others, it seems, may be starting to think so. Philip Pullman, author of *His Dark Materials*, in a review of an exhibition of magic put on in August 2018 by the Ashmolean Museum in Oxford, casts an interested and informed eye over the wide perspective of what he calls, without wishing "to disparage or belittle it," the imaginary world: the world of magic, of religion, of poetry, indeed of "everything that touches human life," which he describes as "surrounded by a penumbra of associations, memories, echoes, and correspondences that extend far into the unknown. In this way of seeing things, the world is full of tenuous filaments of meaning, and the very worst way of trying to see these shadowy existences is to shine a light on them."[1] He is speaking here of the light of scientific reason, but there are other and kinder lights that can be trained on these areas of human experience.

Question and Answer

Asking questions is, surely, one of the few essentials that define being human. The young of animals learn by observing and copying, and by being disciplined and kept in their places by elders and siblings. Children do likewise, but they also initiate: Why? why? why? they ask, as soon as language has provided the magic word. The traditional tales, told, enacted, and sung, which for centuries formed their diet, nourished the tendency. The significance of questions asked and unasked, promising and perilous, is a strong current in the ancient wisdom that flows like an underground river through the landscape of our culture. Question and answer are or once were the scholastic's dialectic, the pianist's two hands, chamber

1. *The Guardian*, Saturday, September 2, 2018.

music's conversation, and a recurring pattern in children's games, nursery rhymes, and songs.

> On yonder hill there stands a creature,
> Who she is I do not know.
> I'll go court her for her beauty;
> She must answer Yes or No.

The themes that led an oral existence for centuries before being lifted into literature or demoted to fairy stories often set up scriptural resonances (and of course vice versa). They demand to be read in a not dissimilar way, in that all have deeper meanings behind or beneath the literal. While a child will not spell them out, these meanings may be absorbed subconsciously and become a part of the ground on which that child walks.

In stories, unlike in life, children do not ask the questions, they get asked for answers: impossible, unguessable answers to trick questions—how can anyone guess a name like Rumpelstiltskin? [2] Sometimes the story turns on a threat of failure, which may spell death; sometimes on the promise of a kingdom as reward—the happy-ever-after of the hall-mark ending. These tests invariably fall to the lot of the least likely candidate, the smallest, youngest, and most vulnerable, who just as invariably triumphs, thereby proving that belief in the triumph of good over evil is written not only in the Scriptures but in the world's genes. It is the truth that continues to deny all the available evidence. Such a story in its many variants says to every child, keep going, never give up, you don't have to be big, strong, rich, or top of the class for something good to come—perchance—your way. Every

---

2. Of course in life they get asked for answers later, interminably, at school and beyond, and often for the wrong answers, those that close down further necessary questions.

happy-ever-after tale is making the same point as Yahweh in
Exodus when he brings his undeserving people out of Egypt.
He did it because they were wretched, not because they de-
served it. Even his "saints," Jacob, David, Solomon the Wise,
weren't more deserving than Jack of the Beanstalk—Moses
was the one exception. Fairy tales are in fact more upbeat
than Scripture, which contains a lot of history, and history is
pretty bleak: God is always having to send his prophets to put
new heart into his people. Yet arching over all is the saving
rainbow of the Flood, the drama of the Passover story, and the
forty-year trek to the Promised Land. Moses may die on the
heights overlooking it, but another Savior will come one day
and lead his people across the Jordan. The Old Testament is
the story of hope against hope.

The New Testament brings one fulfillment: the promised
Savior is given and triumphs over death, the ultimate evil. Yet
this does not take place in the literal, rock-hard sense apparently offered in the fairy tale, where the conferral of kingship
on the hero happens here and now—good things in this tradition are *not* for tomorrow. In the course of the New Testament
the land of milk and honey by contrast gets shifted definitively
beyond the horizon; yet the promise holds good, and the triumph, assuming a cosmic dimension, becomes greater, even
when expressed in literal terms for want of better ("The shout
of them that triumph, / The song of them that feast").[3]

Nonetheless a great deal of moral ambiguity is tolerated
in the Old Testament as in folk tales, even in the doings of the
"goodies," the heroes. There is discomfort in reading about
Jacob's cheating his twin brother Esau out of his blessing and
lying brazenly to his blind father while his mother eggs him on,
and worse discomfort when we realize that his very own God,
the God of Abraham, Isaac, and Jacob, will not hold it against

3. Bernard of Cluny, "Jerusalem the Golden," trans. J. M. Neale.

him. The just God, who insists on the highest standards of integrity in all his people's dealings, appears to turn a blind eye to treachery in his favorite. Yet these stories of the Patriarchs in the book of Genesis, which display an ambiguity in regard to moral issues that is characteristic of primitive tale-telling, tell on another level a different truth to those with ears to hear. They speak of the infinite patience of God with those whom he has chosen to work out his purposes and bring his stories to their redemptive ending. Jacob, after grasping his father's blessing, finds it gets him nowhere without that of the God with whom he has at last to wrestle. He comes out of this contest blessed, but badly lamed, and only then is he given a new name and allowed to return to the Promised Land. These tales are a record of the first tentative steps on a long spiritual journey. The Fathers stepped round the discomfort generated by a proportion of Old Testament stories by reading them metaphorically and have left us a treasure house of scriptural interpretation. Theirs too is a reading between the lines, just as the medieval glosses literally were, lines within lines upon the page, like part-singing, with each voice maintaining its own tune.

The moral elasticity of these tales distinguishes them also from the legendary matter that comes to us already graced with a literary pedigree and firm cultural parameters. The heroes of epics and Arthurian romances are not jumped-up shepherd boys but nobles steeped in honor. Roland at Roncevaux, heavily outnumbered, puts a rearguard at risk because to call for help would demean him. Too late he blows his horn, bursting his temple with the effort; he dies, but so do all his companions. Yet even the wrong choice is presented wrapped in the tragic grandeur that mantles the doings of the Greeks.

But the Hebrew Scriptures are far from uniform, and as we turn the pages the picture changes: the oral component slips beneath the surface, Yahweh moves center stage and takes over. What he expects from his people becomes much more clearly defined, and while their behavior does not necessarily improve (see David's elimination of the inconvenient Uriah[4]), those who transgress are left in no doubt about the consequences. Somewhat surprisingly, moral complexity, if not ambiguity, returns with the Son of God in the gospel parables. Here too is material drawn from the everyday and mediated to the man in the street, and as with fairy tales, the learned today are still working out the meaning of these stories. So are the rest of us, those who have not given up. Why was the dishonest steward / middle manager commended by his master?[5] Why, oh, why are those who have nothing to be deprived even of what they have?[6] I have listened to explanations and forgotten as many as I have heard; perhaps it is better to be wise than to be learned, perhaps the point of the parables lies not in catching the hare, but in continuing the pursuit.

We find a perfect folk tale in the unlikely context of the first Book of Kings: "The Lord appeared to Solomon in a dream and said, 'Ask what you would like me to give you.'"[7] In folklore the unconditional offer is the prerogative of those who, as here, have everything to give, and is frequently qualified with "half my kingdom," which is the same as saying "anything you want" or "wealth beyond your dreams." Alternatively it can be the quid pro quo of some demiurge, engaged in a trade-off with one who has acquired by chance or guile an unlooked-for advantage. There is usually a catch, and the beneficiary who is in line to win everything may end up with nothing. In all such stories excessive greed gets its due requital. Solomon, in asking for wisdom, shows himself wise before the event: courteous and self-deprecating, he asks for a gift that is sure to meet with the approval of the giver. Indeed, when Christ

4. 2 Sam 11.
5. Luke 16:1-13.
6. Matt 13:12; 25:29; Mark 4:25; Luke 19:26.
7. 1 Kgs 3:5-12.

said that to those that have, more would be given, he might have had Solomon in mind.[8]

So-called fairy tales were never the preserve of children, but of the eternal child that lives in all of us and that we suppress at our peril. Unless you become like little children, there is not much hope for you, said Jesus, without specifying clearly which childhood traits he had in mind. Homilists have focused on trustful dependence, a state that tends towards the obedience we like to see in children and used to whip into them, finding that it rarely came of nature. Jesus knew that children are also risk takers, resourceful, truth seers and truth sayers, the only ones to shout that the emperor has no clothes. Much of what we hear or read today, on page or screen or in the press, is less true than we think; our problem with Scripture is that most of it is truer than we can imagine. Perhaps we need to become as little children by returning to Looking-Glass Land.

The Power of the Name

The answer to the trick question in the well-known tale of Rumpelstiltskin, said to go back some four thousand years, is the name of the "manikin" who sets the challenge. A name holds the secret of identity, and to know the name of someone was long thought to confer power. Calling by name implies an assumption that the person will come, like the child Samuel, summoned by the Lord out of sleep by the repetition of his name, "Samuel, Samuel."

The power inherent in a person's name affected nomenclature and modes of address at different times and in different societies. In the knightly class the baptismal name was rarely used among social equals, title, status, or the general "Good Sir" being deemed more appropriate, even between close

---

8. Matt 13:11-12.

friends. The hero of Chrétien de Troyes's last, most enigmatic, and most influential work is nameless when the poem opens ("Dear Son," "Dear Brother," "Good Master" are the names he recognizes and answers to), and when he at last discovers that he is Perceval of Wales, he is immediately demoted to Perceval the Wretched for having failed the test of the unasked question in the first quest he threw himself into after arriving at King Arthur's court.

In Hebrew society equality before God pre-empted other distinctions, and the first thing we learn about a person is the name, which now carries not worldly power, but spiritual, as Saint Matthew makes plain: "She will conceive in her womb and bear a son and you shall call him Jesus, for he shall save his people from their sins":[9] the name speaks for the child before the child is able to speak, and all his forefathers speak for him in turn, starting with Abraham in Matthew and with Adam according to Luke. Since our given name carries meaning, and our roles, our calling, and our spiritual state may change in the course of our lives, Scripture offers examples of names that follow suit. Abram becomes Abraham to mark God's promise of the birth of a son to his wife Sarah, a son who would make him the father of many nations.[10] Simon bar Jonah, equally significantly, by acknowledging the divinity of Christ acquires a new name: he becomes Peter, the rock on which the Lord will build his Church. He remains Simon to his Master throughout Saint John's gospel; it is only in Acts, after the birth of the Church at Pentecost, that he experiences his own resurrection as Peter. All the "victorious," we are told, are to follow one day in his wake, and will each receive a white stone bearing his or her new name—we shall discover who we are.[11]

9. Matt 1:21.
10. Gen 17:4-6.
11. Rev 2:17.

In folk tales most of the figures are characterized only by category or class: the peasant, the prince, the miller, the beast, the witch. Children, mainly girls, are the exceptions: Hansel, Gretel, Jack, Rapunzel, Snow White, Beauty, Goldilocks, Little Red Riding Hood, Cinderella. But these are no less stereotypical. Hansel and Gretel—diminutives for Johann and Margarete, among the commonest names of their day—are Everyboy and Everygirl; the other names define a place in society, a place that magic, grace, luck, resourcefulness will enable the child to escape from. Somewhere there is a rabbit hole, a wardrobe, a way into Looking-Glass Land, where the beast is beautiful and randomness dances hand-in-hand with order. Scripture knows all about Looking-Glass Land, where the eternal child acknowledges its dependence on the great Djinn enthroned on the cloud of providence, dispenser of milk and honey, of grace and glory and bliss-ever-after. In both traditions the way is hard and dangerous and great trust and perseverance are demanded.

Jesus' name was given to his parents and through them to us when he was yet unborn. But we are so slow to understand, and God is so strangely hard to recognize, that the question was still being put and answered when he had passed through death and hell: "Who are you, Lord?" To Thomas, looking at the wounds (surely the most unimaginable aspect of the recently crucified body), he had become "Lord and God," but to Saul on the road the Risen One announces himself simply as the man, Jesus: the man for others, persecuted now *in* others.[12] The men of this generation were the lucky ones; they could ask questions of the two natures, though they found it problematic. Their simpler forebears had been more straightforward but got more baffling answers. Manoah, the father of Samson, is rebuffed by the angel of the Lord: "Why do you

12. Acts 9:5.

ask my name, seeing it is wonderful?"[13] The angel with whom Jacob wrestled all night, and whom he later suggests was the Lord himself, is even less communicative. The divine is not to be named or presumed on as a source of power by humankind; it is of another essence, and this essence is unknowable.

To Moses alone did God utter his name and show something of his glory, once on Mount Horeb when he revealed himself as unknowable essence of being, "I am who am" (Moses never confides this to the children of Israel, who were not ready for a God who is beyond naming—we have not made much progress since), and again on Sinaï, when he proclaimed himself as Yahweh and passed in a cloud before him.[14] Knowing and seeing go together, like the pairing of knowledge and love. To us God in his essence remains past knowing, beyond sight. The longing for the face of God echoes through the Psalms like a refrain and has furnished prayer and meditation ever since: "It is your face, O Lord, that I seek, / hide not your face."[15] "My soul is thirsting for God, the living God, / when can I enter and see / the face of God?"[16]

The Risen Christ

Yet since Bethlehem, we, his new people, know the Father in a new way, in the incarnate Son.[17] But is seeing him in Jesus the same as seeing him in Old Testament terms? Would Moses have settled for that? Did Philip, who had just been reproved for asking to be shown the Father, feel satisfied with what he was offered? Perhaps he saw it at the time as an evasion at the time but came to understand it later. All the disciples, not just Thomas, had a problem with the risen body, a problem

13. Judg 13:18.
14. Exod 34:6.
15. Ps 27:8.
16. Ps 42:2.
17. John 14:8.

they, despite their best efforts, have passed on to us, and just because it is the pivot of our faith,[18] it is also a stumbling block. What does a risen body look like? Something no one had ever seen and the disciples had no words for. Mary Magdalene took him for a gardener (was he perhaps holding a spade?).[19] Luke, striving to explain why the two on the way to Emmaus failed to recognize him despite the time spent walking and talking, writes that he "showed himself under a different form."[20]

One might be reading a fairy tale; this is not a hundred miles from the Frog Prince or Beauty's Beast or any other of the many forms in which the Lover is temporarily hidden from the eyes of a Beloved left to persevere in patient service, often with no promise of a happy outcome. And nor did the disciples get any better at it: those who had been present in the upper room when he passed through the closed door failed again in Galilee to recognize him on the lake shore. Perhaps the risen Christ was just too ordinary, the perfect illustration of the expression "invisible in plain sight." Everyman is no man and every man, different each time we meet him. The moment of recognition comes later, suddenly, when all are looking away, and the unknown stranger *acts*: speaks a name, starts to prepare a meal,[21] breaks bread.[22] He is known in the instant of connection, the current of relationship. Ascended now and omnipresent (another word used to mask a black hole in our understanding), he confers a new form of blessing on us, his latter-day faithful who have not seen, or heard, or touched, but yet believe.[23] Or do we? The wounds only figure once in

18. 1 Cor 15:14.
19. John 20:15.
20. Luke 24:14-15.
21. John 21:9. John has already recognized him when the net fills with fish.
22. Luke 24:30-31.
23. John 20:29.

the resurrection stories, when Thomas demands to see them as proof that it is he. In every other appearance the risen Lord seems strangely unmarked:

> I think that you'll agree in any light
> You'd never spot the scars about my head.

The poet Charles Causley, past master of the in-between language, knows so well our weak points and what makes us ill at ease:

> "We all agree," they said, "you're looking spry,
> But is that blood that's running down your wrists?"

The onlookers referred to here are not the apostles, but us in the "world of men":

> He lost the old, the eloquent appeal.
> Friends looked away, and love finally died,
> For who, touching the Bridegroom, cares to feel
> Holes in the hands and feet, except the Bride?[24]

Perhaps the wounds in the risen body were only visible to those who had a longing to see them. We say that Christ entered heaven bearing in his body the wounds which are his and ours; this is the language of need, the small talk of love, that gets christened mystical theology. It takes a poet to give it form.

Fluidity of Time and Space

The Acts of the Apostles, which has the appearance on one level of a historical narrative, is peppered with unaccountable happenings: miraculous healings, visions, escapes from jails locked and guarded; it is as though, post-Pentecost, a fourth dimension had been opened up, reserved until then to angels, which properly belong there. One of these beings allegedly spoke to the deacon Philip, saying, "Set out at noon and go along the road that leads from Jerusalem down to Gaza, the

---

24. Charles Causley, "After The Accident," *Collected Poems 1951–1997* (London: Macmillan, 1992), 152.

desert road." So far, so specific. There he met a eunuch in the service of the queen of Ethiopia. After a most productive conversation the eunuch, noticing some water not far off, asked to be baptized, and "after they had come up out of the water again Philip was taken away by the Spirit of the Lord," while the eunuch "went on his way rejoicing." Philip, with no apparent interval, "appeared in Azotus."[25]

Saint Luke is pointing us here towards Elijah whisked up to heaven in the whirlwind,[26] to indicate an occurrence he cannot otherwise explain. Bi-location, telepathy: here we are on terrain familiar from folk tales and hagiography, which witnesses down the centuries, both credible and less credible, have claimed as part of their experience. In modern times such claims have been generally dismissed, though recent developments in physics may be approaching the phenomena from another direction. Meanwhile they can be spoken of only in the language of faith and myth and fairy tale, the language that sees no barriers between time and eternity, and space as telescopic.

Myth, legend, fairy tale offer a common language for reading Scripture—a language long familiar and never quite lost, a language that grew out of story-telling, and stories are never cut and dried. A good story consists of narrative, theme, and meaning. The narrative is the piper's tune to gather us, the listeners, and carry us along. The theme is the context, it embodies the meaning. The meaning is the wisdom of the tribe, the people, the society, of the human heart and spirit, distilled over time. Pipers succeed one another, often compete, playing the same tunes, but with variations, and each claims loudly that his rendering is better, indeed truer than the others, the *only* true version, true to the spirit—or in the case of Scripture, to the Spirit. The problem with Scripture

25. Acts 8:26-40.
26. 2 Kgs 2:11.

is that it encapsulates truths that are past our imagining—I note that Philip Pullman, as quoted earlier, leaves the word *imaginary* conveniently undefined.

There is a misfit too between faith and belief, which we tend mistakenly to put in the same box. "Oh you of little faith!" is the reproach repeatedly leveled by Jesus at his disciples. It is lack of faith that lies at the root of Peter's betrayal,[27] no doubt of Judas's too. Faith is spatial, not linear like belief: a bed-sit for settling into and moving around in. Its furniture has been given—fine pieces, hand-made by an excellent carpenter. All that we have brought to it are the rarely read books on the shelves and a knick-knackery of prayers and hymns and good intentions scattered round about. Faith is for living in, with Another, in deepening familiarity and trust. Men and women die for articles of the creed; in faith they live. A fictional motel cleaner makes the distinction clear: "Nobody was allowed to be fully certain about God. And she'd never trusted anybody who claimed to be certain about God. You cannot be confident and faithful at the same time, she thought."[28]

The language of myth and fairy tale is also that of poetry, open-ended, tolerant of more than one interpretation and which allows us, for a time, to redefine possibility, in the way we suspend disbelief in the theater. The Evangelists had no problem here, as they could refer back to the highest authority: "With man this is impossible, but with God all things are possible."[29] It is the language used by those who find no words—no syntax above all—to explain their experience, often private, sometimes shared. The failure is not theirs but an inadequacy of the tools at their disposal. If something utterly new takes place, a language based on experience is bound

27. Luke 22:32.

28. Sherman Alexie, "Clean, Cleaner, Cleanest," www.newyorker.com/magazine/2017/06/05/clean-cleaner-cleanest.

29. Matt 19:26.

to fall short. The disciples rendered what they saw and heard in the words that they had; they put these words together as tradition had taught them, and if the results expanded the universe, so be it; their God wanted his new wine in new skins. Their prophets, who had already spoken in cryptic language that nobody objected to, were now perceived to be ferrying in their words a new and explosive meaning: the road to Emmaus changed everything.

Witnesses, like children, are expected be truth-tellers, it is the only thing required of them. And these were faithful to that calling, continuing to repeat in simple words the simple, inexplicable things they had seen. "Yes, there were a few loaves, and yes, fewer fish, but everybody had enough. The really remarkable thing was the left-overs: baskets and baskets of the lavishness of God." It doesn't make sense? "It did to us," they said, "—after he rose again." But they didn't make literature of it; they left that to us. They used the only language they knew, the one that is gloriously simple with the simplicity that knows no limits, that stretches to outer space and beyond. We, with our cheap-jack taste for complication, have often turned it into literature.

This language followed men and women into the desert. The best lives of the saints are written in it (hagiographers, alas, can do literature too). Historians shy away from it, and the Enlightenment Zeitgeist finds it risible. Julian of Norwich and her like are at home in it. The Church often struggles with it, wary of the high-wire act and preferring the spurious safety of extremes, while rejecting the paradox that enables them. Scripture scholars pick at it, professional theologians favor an abstruse dialect, which few outsiders understand. The in-between language survives, but is rarely found in the mainstream. It helps to be fluent in it if we wish to recognize the Spirit at work in our lives, surprising us at every turn.

Lightning Source UK Ltd.
Milton Keynes UK
UKHW011848090420
361578UK00001B/15